LEARNING A
MUSICAL
INSTRUMENT

A Guide for Adult Learners

Richard Crozier

ROBERT HALE

First published in 2016 by Robert Hale,
an imprint of The Crowood Press Ltd,
Ramsbury, Marlborough Wiltshire SN8 2HR

www.crowood.com

www.halebooks.com

British Library Cataloguing-in-Publication Data
A catalogue record for this book is available from the British
Library.

ISBN 978 0 7198 1616 1

Typeset by Jean Cussons Typesetting, Diss, Norfolk

Printed and bound in India by Replika Press Pvt Ltd

Contents

Introduction

This guide is for adults of all ages who are thinking about taking up a musical instrument for the first time, or who are picking up from where they left off while at school. It addresses the questions that may be in the mind of the would-be learner, such as:

- Which instrument should I choose?
- How do I find a good teacher?
- Will I be able to do it?
- Will learning music be too hard for me?
- How much will it all cost?

Learning an instrument from scratch or resuming music lessons is one of the most absorbing and exciting things anyone can do, and need hold no fear for you if you are willing to give it a go. The rewards will be numerous, without doubt.

Music exists in a huge number of different formats across almost all cultural groups, but the focus in this volume is principally on instruments used in Western classical music-making, with jazz and popular music included, and a brief look at traditional instruments and some from Indian classical music. The book includes practical information about all the commonly taught instruments, the real stories of some individuals who have taken up an instrument, a look at music education, and a glossary of terms used. Also included are a recommended reading list and compilation of web addresses for some of the many associations and organizations connected with music that are based in the UK.

CHAPTER 1

Starting your Musical Journey

STARTING FROM SCRATCH OR PICKING UP THE THREADS

Perhaps you are one of those people who have never really experienced the joy of music, but just feel that you know instinctively that it is worth finding out some more about it – or maybe you began engaging in some form of music-making when you were at school, but for all sorts of reasons it has just dropped out of your life, or you chose to drop it from your regular pattern of activities.

Music makes human beings human: it is a much older form of communication than reading and writing, and it deals directly with your emotions, rather than facts or information about them. It is a form of self-expression that can also be a form of communication. As a form of communication it has the advantage of allowing you, as a composer, to 'say' what you want to say, but it also allows the listener to 'hear' what they want to hear, and allows a performer to make the music express what they want it to express. There is no other art form that works in quite the same way as music, because music only exists while it is being performed and while you listen to it. The rest of the time it may be stored in another format, such as digitally, on vinyl, on CD or on paper, but you can only hear it when it is performed or when a recording of it is played.

It really doesn't matter if you are not a great performer: the important thing is that you make music at your own level. The reality is that even the greatest performers and composers weren't great when they started – even child prodigies had to begin somewhere. As you begin to learn music through playing or singing you will gain a heightened awareness of the attainment of greater performers, and an insight into what the greatest performers are capable of.

So, let's begin with a few questions to provoke some thinking and get the ball rolling:

- Do you remember your class music lessons from your school days?

- Do you remember more of music in your primary or your secondary school?
- Did you enjoy your music lessons?
- Can you recall anything musical that you learnt from those lessons?
- Did you take part in any musical groups in school time?
- Did you take part in any music-making out of school?
- Do you listen to music now? If you do, is it live or recorded?
- Do you take part in any form of music-making now?
- Do you sometimes imagine yourself playing a musical instrument. If so, which one?
- What sort of music do you like: jazz, pop, classical, world, other?

In conversation adults are often heard to say that they wish they had been given the opportunity to learn a musical instrument, or that they had persevered with the instrument they did start learning when they were at school. This book will help you if those thoughts are in your mind, or if you just have an idea that you'd like to make some music. There's no reason why anyone shouldn't be able to make reasonable progress learning an instrument, especially with the help of a good teacher and some time dedicated to practise. After all, playing, composing and listening to music are natural and enjoyable activities, and learning to play music well on an instrument, or taking part in some sort of choral group, should also be an enjoyable activity, and will be, if the teaching style and instrument are right for you, the learner. If you started lessons at school but didn't get very far, why not give it another go and see if you can take it a few steps further?

In the past, learning music in a school environment often meant learning information about music. It is much easier for music teachers to teach factual information about composers, pieces of music, musical notation, musical theory, instruments and so on, than to get a whole class of children involved in practical music-making. And in one sense it is easier for learners to learn this way, and then to be tested on whether they have remembered the facts they have been given. Unfortunately that sort of teaching and learning does nothing to satisfy our natural desire to *make* music of whatever kind we choose. Sadly, many people remember more about the less musical aspects of their musical encounters at school, and in contrast remember the joy, delight and excitement of discovering and following, say, pop music, which they did for themselves, and from which they took enjoyment as much by being listeners as participants.

This book is all about encouraging you to embrace practical music-making in whatever musical genre appeals most to you, regardless of any of your musical experiences in the past.

If your experience of classroom music was less than wholly positive, or if you began learning to play an instrument but lost interest, or had too much pressure on your time, then there is no better time than the present to put things right. Whatever style of music appeals to you, and whichever instrument you would like to play, there's no reason to hold back from having a go. You can learn a lot about music through learning to make and control sounds on an instrument, without wanting, or being able to be, the greatest performing musician on that instrument. Once you get started, you may find that your interest moves more towards composition, or towards working with sounds electronically. Effective instrumental teachers teach music through the instrument, rather than just teaching the technique that you need in order to play the instrument itself.

Learning to play an instrument describes the journey from simply making a sound, to acquiring control over sound and tone production, fluency as a performer, and in many cases, confidently reading written musical notation. Perhaps very few people, if any, truly complete the journey, but whether you progress just a few steps along the way, or enjoy some truly long-haul travel, it should bring you enormous satisfaction. This book provides some information and suggestions to help anyone who is embarking on that journey.

DOES AGE MATTER?

When it comes to learning to play a musical instrument, age really does not matter. Starting the violin or piano at the age of five does mean that your fingers are more flexible, and yes, it does get a little harder, in that respect, the older you are – but the compensating advantage of age is being able to understand why it's a little more difficult, and knowing how to pace yourself on your learning journey. It is most certainly never too late. When it comes to your choice of instrument, rather than focusing on its size or shape, it may be as helpful and important to focus on your gut reaction to the sound and sight of the instrument, and the music you have heard being made on it. There is research evidence to show that individuals with certain temperaments are more likely to be suited to particular instruments, so don't be afraid of being guided by your feelings and intuition, as well as keeping an eye on some of the practicalities.

It may be that you are simply picking up the threads from what you learned whilst you were at school, or this may be a completely new adventure for you. In either case, there's nothing to stop you, and no reason to hold back. As with anything new in life, the old saying that 'every journey starts with the first step', holds true. Once you have taken that first step, there is no reason at all why you shouldn't travel a long way in your exploration of one of the most intriguing and fascinating art forms there is, and the speed of your journey is not the most important thing.

There may be a number of practical matters that need careful consideration, but let's begin by looking at what music is, how the sounds of music are made, and what the positive benefits of learning music are.

WHAT IS MUSIC?

Music is harder to define than it first appears. We cannot see it, touch it, smell it or taste it. We can liken it to natural sounds or the sound of an animal or human voice, but we perceive it differently from the way we perceive colour, for example. When it is played or performed, each individual component sound of a piece of music only lasts as long as the composer and the performer require it to, after which it is replaced by another sound. We may describe a musical work as lasting three minutes, or thirty minutes, or three hours, but unless there are one or more sustained sounds throughout, the individual sounds are momentary. Furthermore on many instruments the sounds naturally diminish from the first sounding of the note. In its notated form (called the score), music in one sense does appear to become more tangible, and someone with acute aural perception may be able to hear a complete symphony in their head, simply by looking at its notation.

For most people music has a temporary existence, akin to spoken language, and in one sense it does not exist other than as a passing experience. It is this quality that makes music what it is, and whilst we have developed all kinds of sophisticated recording mechanisms allowing us access to almost any piece of music of our choosing, and the ability to listen to it as many times as we choose in almost any circumstances, there is no real substitute for the live performance of music. It is only through live performance that we really experience the power of music, the power that drew us towards it in the first place.

As an art form, music is found in almost every human culture, and exists in many different forms. It carries a huge array of functions, including dance, ceremonial, ritual, accompaniment, as a mirror to human emotions, such as at a wedding or a funeral, and having meaning in its own right. It is performed by professional musicians, who are paid to perform, semi-professionals and amateurs alike. It is found throughout history as being important to almost all societies, and remains so today.

Music is sometimes referred to as an international language. It is of course a non-verbal language, and conveys emotion and meaning to the listener through its structure, harmony, instrumentation and performance. It is because it is non-verbal that mastery in one sense presents a greater challenge to the learner: in verbal language you can easily test your achievement and attainment in practical or theoretical terms. In music-making you may perform well in terms of getting the sounds right, and may even pass all your graded exams, but you may still fail to ignite the spark that is communication, and which is the very essence of music-making.

SOURCES OF MUSICAL SOUNDS

Sound is created by the vibration of air or materials, and musical instruments can be categorized according to the way sound is produced on them. In the Western classical tradition, instruments are grouped in families such as those found in the symphony orchestra: strings, woodwind, brass, percussion and keyboard.

A more widely applicable categorization was developed in the early twentieth century in which the group names are aerophones, chordophones, idiophones, membranophones and electrophones. Percussion instruments, or those that you hit or strike to produce a sound, are found in two groups: idiophones and membranophones. However, early percussion instruments are known to have been lithophones or, in other words, rocks or pieces of rock that were struck to produce a particular sound. Brasswind and woodwind instruments are categorized as aerophones, stringed instruments as chordophones. Electronic instruments are referred to as electrophones. For most people, understanding the categories is not of particular importance because they are most likely to be interested primarily in one, or a few, specific instruments. There is a full list at the end of this chapter.

The characteristic sounds produced by a vibrating column of air, or material, are determined by the frequencies it produces. The tuning fork that a piano tuner or sometimes a choirmaster uses, vibrates predominantly at a single frequency producing a clear, quiet sound, whereas a clarinet produces more complex vibrations and a set of frequencies which give it its characteristic sound. This character is referred to as the *timbre* of the instrument, and the difference in vibrating frequencies accounts for the difference between, say, a flute and a clarinet, or a bassoon and a trombone. It is probable that certain timbres will appeal to you more than others, so if you are not sure about which instrument you would like to play, try and listen to as many as you can and allow your heart to rule your head – unless you find yourself settling on an instrument that is just going to be impractical for you.

MUSIC'S COMPONENTS

Music consists of pitch, volume, rhythm, harmony, texture and timbre, and when a sound is made, we speak of its attack, how well it sustains itself, and its decay.

Let's take a moment and explore these terms in the context of learning to play a musical instrument or developing vocal skills. Pitch is fairly self-explanatory, and by creating sounds of differing pitch we are able to construct and recall a melody. The volume at which we play any of our sounds is likewise easy to understand, and in Western classical musical notation we use Italian terms such as forte (loud) and *piano* (soft or quiet) to describe and refer to these musical volumes or dynamics, and these terms are quickly acquired and mastered. Rhythm refers to the sequence of one sound after another when set against a pulse of some sort, and plays a significant part in the way that we are able to memorize music. Harmony occurs when two or more sounds are played or sung together. Timbre is simply the characteristic sound of one instrument or voice compared with another: for example the timbre of the saxophone is different to that of the clarinet and the violin.

When we make sounds musically we learn to control or influence all of these component factors. Similarly we learn to begin sounds in different ways to reflect the composer's wishes, to sustain the sounds in particular ways, and to let the sounds die away or decay in different ways. All this is done to turn the composer's notation into music and to develop our own interpretation of the composition before us, so that we are able to communicate our own version of the composer's wishes. Some instruments, for example woodwind and brasswind, allow us to maintain loud sound for the duration of a long-held note, as long as our breath control permits. On bowed strings we can similarly maintain a loud sound, but on the piano the sound begins to die away from the moment the key is struck. Learning to play music musically involves developing the necessary skills to control or influence all these factors.

Playing Off Key, Tuning and Intonation

It is not unusual to hear someone describe a musical performance as being 'off key', meaning that it wasn't enjoyable to listen to and sounded wrong in some way. Most Western music is written in a particular key, chosen by the composer. It could be a major or a minor key, and a key signature will be written at the beginning of each line of music. For all keys, other than C major and A minor, this means there will be a number of sharp or flat signs, although never mixed, placed at the beginning of each musical stave, and the performer must remember to implement these sharps or flats as he or she plays the piece. In one sense, playing 'off key' could simply mean forgetting to sharpen or flatten a particular note, and this would certainly make the piece sound incorrect.

However, the term is sometimes – perhaps mistakenly – used to describe playing that is out of tune. Western musical instruments manufactured in recent times are all designed and constructed to be played at the pitch where the note A (A above Middle C on the piano, or the pitch that is found in the second space up in the treble clef) is tuned to 440hz: this is sometimes referred to as 'concert pitch'. The fixing of A=440hz was only agreed formally in the middle of the last century, so is a relatively recent innovation. The term 'concert pitch' is also used in the context of transposing instruments, such as the clarinet, trumpet or saxophone, where an instrument, such as the clarinet pitched in B flat, actually produces sounds one whole tone lower than the player is reading. The sound produced is referred to by conductors and players as being at concert pitch, in order to be clear exactly what is being discussed during a rehearsal.

Although an instrument may be constructed to sound A=440hz, it is still down to the player to play that instrument in tune. For example, a piano that is left untuned will slip out of tune as some of the strings slacken with the effects of temperature fluctuations and so on, and some notes will sound flat. In this case it is the piano tuner's job to tune the piano as perfectly as possible, and the owner's job to keep the piano regularly tuned. In the case of a woodwind instrument, the player could make small adjustments in pitch by altering the overall length of the tube, for example, pushing the mouthpiece or reed further in, or pulling it out a small amount. Even having done this, the player can raise or lower the pitch of a note when playing simply by the way he or she makes the sounds. These small differences in pitch, smaller than a semitone, are referred to as poor intonation.

A comment about someone's poor intonation may override the fact that they have played the piece at an appropriate speed, taken note of the key signature, and played expressively with suitable dynamics and a good dynamic range – but if, nevertheless, they have played some notes flatter or sharper than they should be, they would still be playing with poor intonation. We may describe a player as having poor intonation because the pitch of the notes is inconsistent. It is sometimes these inconsistencies in pitching that result in the description 'off key', even though the player believes that they are playing all the correct notes and sharpening or flattening notes according to the key signature's instructions.

The need for an agreed fixed pitch is centred on the desire to play music together on different instruments. In Elizabethan times instruments tended to be played more in family groups of instruments, so a group of different sized recorders might be played together and would very probably have all been made by the same maker and tuned to a specific pitch. A neighbour's recorders may have come from a different maker and be tuned to a slightly higher or lower pitch, so it would not have been possible to play all the instruments together with a harmonious effect.

Before the nineteenth century there were few attempts to standardize musical pitch, and levels across Europe varied widely, not just from place to place or over time, but often within the same locality and by as much as four or five semitones. Pitch was set by tuning forks, from which an instrument tuner may still take their starting note today, but these could also be manufactured to sound different pitches for supposedly the same note.

For many years, pitch was increased by players seeking to get a brighter sound from their instruments, and instrument makers simply responded to this demand. While this may be acceptable for instrumentalists, it was bad for singers who experienced difficulty reaching their higher notes, and for some stringed instruments where the necessary tightening of the strings caused too much additional tension within the instrument.

Playing in tune and with good intonation takes time and practice. For the pianist it is simply a matter of making sure that the instrument you are using is tuned regularly, and that's an end of it. For all other musicians it's a question of developing both the practical skills to ensure that you are reading and playing the correct note, and alongside those, developing the necessary aural skills to ensure that you are creating and sustaining that note in tune. When playing with others it is often necessary to compensate, so that if your fellow performers play sharper or flatter you can tune your playing to them, rather than to a fixed external pitch.

When two instruments are being played together, other than

agreeing to tune to A=440hz, one instrument being played sharp simply makes the other one sound flat. Temperature and acoustics both contribute to pitch differences, so this adds a further layer of complexity. A good teacher will help you, as a beginner, to acquire the skill to listen to your own sound and that of others, and to adjust your intonation accordingly, having tuned your instrument to a fixed external pitch to begin with.

MUSIC-MAKING IS 'GOOD FOR YOU'

If you are already thinking about taking up an instrument or joining a choir, you probably don't need too much more encouragement, but it may help you to know that there is a wealth of evidence to support the view that music itself, and in particular taking part in music-making, is a good thing for pleasure, health and well-being.

Music has been part of human culture for many years. It was probably part of the cultural change which took place in Europe between 60,000 and 30,000 years ago. Simple bone flutes dating from some 43,000 years ago lead us to assume that the techniques of making instruments and playing music were passed down via an oral tradition for generations, and if we take a brief look back at more recent history it tells us that there are numerous references to the value of music. Here are just a few: the Chinese philosopher Confucius (551–479BC) said in *The Book of Rites*, 'Music produces a kind of pleasure which human nature cannot do without.' In ancient Greece, music played an important part in society. Around 500BC, Pythagoras studied the musical scale and the ratios between the lengths of vibrating strings needed to produce them. He articulated a theory of harmony and proportion which connected music, sound, colour and light. Another Greek philosopher, Plato, born around 425BC, referred frequently to music in his writings.

It is believed that the development of Western musical notation occurred in the Church across various parts of Europe. Many of the earliest forms of musical notation were for choral music, with the notes being typically indicated above the word or syllable of the text being sung. The church music of this period is known as 'Plainchant' or 'Gregorian chant', and is named after Pope Gregory, who was pope from approximately 590 until his death in 604AD. Precise note pitches were not specified in the notation used at this time: it was simply a matter of whether a note should be higher or lower than the previous one. In England, the earliest schools that we know anything about date from around 600AD, and included music as part of the curriculum.

A stave of four lines, similar in appearance to the five-line stave we use today, is usually attributed to the Italian, Guido d'Arezzo (c991–1033), and from the thirteenth century a way of indicating rhythm was also developed. Slowly, with the four-line stave being increased to five lines, what we recognize as modern musical notation developed. The introduction of clefs to indicate the range of sounds shown on a stave became accepted, and as keyboard instruments were pioneered, so was the idea of using two separate clefs, one for each hand, for music composed specially for keyboard.

Music played a prominent part in Elizabethan England, when it became more refined and sophisticated. New musical forms, including the madrigal and ayre, and instruments, including the viol, were introduced. Music in this period became more expressive overall, and the court of Elizabeth I and the homes of the nobility featured music and entertainment from musicians. New instruments included the viol, the hautboy, a precursor to the oboe, and a number of keyboard instruments including the spinet, the harpsichord and the virginal. Elizabethan composers did not insist which instruments should be used to play the music they composed, but left that decision to those who played their compositions.

Perhaps the best known composer of the Elizabethan era is William Byrd (c.1540–1623), who served as an organist and chorister of the Chapel Royal. Arguably the most prolific and most versatile English composer of the era, Byrd wrote hundreds of pieces over six decades, including masses, motets (songs for multiple voices without instruments), liturgical music, secular songs for solo voice and small vocal ensembles, pieces for keyboard and for strings, and instrumental fantasias. Of particular interest to us is the preface to his *Psalmes, Sonnets & Songs*, published in 1588, in which he gave eight reasons for his belief in the value of singing:

1. It is a knowledge easely taught and quickly learned, where there is a good Master and an apt Scoller.
2. The exercise of singing is delightfull to Nature and good to preserve the health of Man.
3. It doth strengthen all parts of the brest, and doth open the pipes.
4. It is a singular good remedie for stammering in the speech.
5. It is the best meanes to procure a perfect pronunciation, and to make a good Orator.
6. It is the onely way to know where Nature hath bestowed the benefit of a good voyce; which guift is so rare as there is not one among a thousand that hath it; and in many that excellent guift is lost because they want Art to express Nature.

7. There is not any Musicke of Instruments whatsoever compara-
ble to that which is made of the voyces of men, where the voyces
are good and the same well sorted and ordered.

8. The better the voyce is, the meter it is to honour and serve God
therewith; and the voyce of man is chiefly to be employed to
that ende.

Since singing is so good a thing,
I wish all men would learne to sing.

Byrd addresses us in the language of his time, but there is little
doubt about his complete dedication to the value of singing. We'll
come back to the idea of starting your journey with your singing
voice later in this book.

In Germany, Bach (1685–1750) described music as 'harmonious
euphony for the glory of God and the instruction of my neighbour'.

Writing in 1888, the German philosopher Nietzsche says, 'Without music, life would be a mistake'; and moving forwards to modern
times, the term 'musicking' was coined by Christopher Small, a
New Zealand-born musician, composer and educator, in his book
of the same name published in 1998. He used the term to explain
his belief that music was a verb, an activity, rather than a noun, and
emphasized the importance of the activity over the notation.

Music educator Professor Keith Swanwick, in his book *Teaching
Music Musically* (*see* Recommended Reading), draws our attention
to the work of an earlier writer, Merriam, who identified music
as being 'good for' the following: emotional expression; aesthetic
enjoyment; entertainment; communication; symbolic representa-
tion; physical response; enforcing conformity to social norms; vali-
dation of social institutions and religious rituals; and as a contribution to the continuity and stability of culture and the preservation
of social integration. Thus with no more than a moment's reflection
it is clear that music plays many roles for us in our everyday lives.

Many people, especially in Western culture, think of, and refer
to musical notation as music, and a focus on notation and studying written music is given pre-eminence in programmes of study at
many levels – whereas Small argues that the real importance lies
in the activity and the sounds that it generates. For our purposes,
it serves as a reminder that there is strong evidence to support the
view that any engagement with music, be it as an active listener,
composer or performer, is beneficial to the health and well-being of
the individual. This idea dates back for many generations, but Small
was among the first to articulate it so clearly in modern times.

Current research has shown that music can help with many things: it can help pain management; it can improve the value of a workout at the gym; help develop areas of the brain involved in language and reasoning; and enhance teamwork skills and discipline – and there are many more good reasons for engaging in musical activity. It is perhaps rather sad to note that, all too often, when music and its place on the school curriculum are being discussed, reference is made to 'the Mozart effect'. This term was coined by the French otolaryngologist, Alfred Tomatis (1920–2001), who used it to describe a slightly different beneficial effect from the one later popularized by Don Campbell in his book *The Mozart Effect*. Campbell claimed benefits relating to the transformational power of music on health and well-being, and in educational outcomes when young children listen to music. Even if the claims are true, and subsequent research has cast some doubt on this, foremost is the joy of 'musicking' in itself, which can bring pleasure to you as the music-maker, and with a rising level of accomplishment and achievement, quickly bring pleasure to your listeners as well. There is abundant evidence to suggest that spending some time learning to make music is indeed time well spent.

As a reminder of the instruments that are available to you, why not take a look at this list. It uses the categories developed in the early twentieth century and the more familiar Western orchestra family groupings as well. Pianos and harpsichords are a little more difficult to categorize. The piano sometimes gets grouped with percussion instruments because when the keys are pressed the hammers hit the strings. It is also grouped with the percussion family in the symphony orchestra. With the harpsichord, the strings are plucked when the keys are depressed.

In the table opposite, instruments are grouped by the way they create sounds.

Woodwind	Brasswind	Strings	Percussion	Percussion	Electronic instruments
aerophones	chordo-phones	idiophones	membrano-phones	electro-phones	
Recorder	Cornet	Violin	Xylophone	Timpani	Guitar
Ocarina	Trumpet	Viola	Cymbals	Snare drum	Bass guitar
Piccolo	Flugelhorn	Cello	Hi-Hats	Bass drum	Keyboard
Flute	French horn	Double bass	Bells	Tom-tom	Synthesizer
Fife	Trombone	Harp	Wood block	Tabla	Electronic organ
Oboe	Tenor horn	Guitar	Singing bowl	Djembe	
Cor anglais	Baritone horn	Balalaika	Steel tongue drum		
Oboe d'amore	Euphonium	Banjo	Triangle		
Clarinet	Tuba	Guitar	Marimba		
Bassoon	Sousaphone	Lute			
Saxophone		Mandolin			
		Sitar			
Accordion		Ukelele			
Concertina					
Harmonium		Piano			
Mouth organ		Harpsichord			
Pipes					

CHAPTER 2

What's Involved in Learning an Instrument

Perhaps somewhere, in a corner of your mind, is the notion that you would like to do something involving music-making. The idea may be quite advanced and you already know which instrument you would like to play. Perhaps you have already pictured yourself making music on this instrument, or maybe the idea is still at that rather vague stage where you need something to steer you a bit more firmly in one direction. If that is the case, then this chapter should help you to make up your mind by approaching the issue from a very pragmatic standpoint.

PERSONAL CONSIDERATIONS

Personal considerations include eyesight, noise, location, musical skills and singing.

Let's once again start with a few simple questions:

- Do you know which instrument you would like to learn?
- Do you have a particular musical style or genre in mind?
- Does your current accommodation allow you to store and play that instrument?
- Might neighbours be an issue in terms of your playing disturbing them?
- Do you wear glasses?
- Are there pets that may be disturbed by musical sounds, in your home or nearby?
- Have you ever done any singing?
- Do you have any physical limitations that might influence your choice of instrument?

Yes, it's a sort of checklist, but it really isn't intended to stop you in your tracks or stifle your enthusiasm for making some music. However, before rushing to your computer to order an instrument over the internet, or dashing to your local music shop, if you're lucky enough still to have one, it may just help to spend a few moments to think about your personal situation and a few practical matters. Where will you keep your instrument? Not too difficult for a flautist, but tricky for a pianist if your home isn't particularly large. Will you be able to practise without disturbing other family members and neighbours? Do you wear glasses, and ones with different focal lengths? Check that you can focus easily on some sheet music on a music stand, and talk to your optician if the dots aren't clear enough for you to see and read comfortably. Do you anticipate any difficulties picking up or holding the instrument you have in mind? Is your breathing all right?

All that said, it's unlikely there will be anything insurmountable that will prevent you from some engagement with practical musical activity, and a little thought in advance should help to smooth the way forwards. In the next few pages we'll take a look at some of the background factors to learning an instrument.

HOW NOISY WILL LEARNING AN INSTRUMENT BE?

Some instruments do generate quite a high volume of sound, particularly in the early stages of learning as you acquire the necessary skills to control and shape the sound, and master your instrument's dynamic range. The trumpet is a good example from the brass family, and the oboe from the woodwind. Violins generate much less volume in the early stages, although the sounds that a beginner makes may not go in the category of sweet music. You will need to consider the impact of regular practice on other members of your household, including pets, as well as your neighbours. For example, dogs may join in enthusiastically with your instrument if the frequency of the instrumental sound is in a particular part of their hearing range, and their howling may be more irritating to your neighbours than the embryonic musical sounds you are coaxing from your instrument.

An upright piano should be located, where practicable, on a non-party wall, out of direct sunlight and away from central-heating radiators. Modern uprights are fitted with a practice pedal that can be locked into position placing a felt bar against the strings to muffle the sound. This is good in many respects, but may have the negative effect that, as a learner, you become used to a sound which is not the really full sound of a piano. Brass instruments can be fitted with a special mute which allows them to be played almost silently, but again this is not ideal for the absolute beginner. Although the conventional drum kit generates a significant amount of sound/noise, there are two substitutes which may help: practice pads, which take the form of rubber discs that are used to help players acquire stick technique, reducing the sound dramatically; and electronic kits, which allow players to hear themselves on headphones while the rest of the world is blissfully unaware of what's going on.

In short, playing a musical instrument, unsurprisingly, makes a sound which at first may be closer to the noise end of the spectrum, but which you will very soon develop into a pleasant musical sound. Most beginners are unlikely to play for more than half an hour a day, so partners, families and pets should simply prepare for this as part of the learning process. If this really does seem too much, serious thought should be given as to whether it is appropriate for you to begin lessons at all – but in almost all circumstances you should be able to find a way to negotiate around these potential difficulties.

MUSICAL AND OTHER SKILLS

Start by asking yourself the following questions:

- If you hear some music playing, can you tap or clap the beat? (Remember the beat is the pulse, not the rhythm – *see* later in this chapter if you're not sure.)
- If you hear a sound, can you hum or sing the same pitch?
- Can you sing a simple tune – it doesn't matter what it is – so that all the notes are at the right pitch? Try singing a tune such as Happy Birthday to You; Twinkle, Twinkle Little Star; Jingle Bells.
- Do you sense that you're getting the notes mostly right if you sing with other people?
- Have you any knowledge of musical theory?

Once again, your answers are less important than, in this case, your ability to start listening to the musical sounds you are making, and to appraise your own performance.

Playing a musical instrument requires the bringing together of a complex set of skills. At one extreme, some individuals seem to take to instrumental learning so naturally it is hard to believe they are picking up the instrument for the first time. Others will find some aspects more difficult, and a few people, but no more than a tiny minority, find the whole thing very challenging. This is where we confront the issues of progress and perseverance for all learners.

An effective teacher will use a range of strategies to encourage you if you are finding something difficult, and help you persevere to overcome these challenges. Progress may be slow in terms of outcomes – playing the music – but here the progress is the satisfaction and success that is found within you, and which should be celebrated just as much as the outward signs of playing the music more fluently.

Your attainment as a musician may be measured by passing music exams. In this case your progress is compared equally with anyone else learning the same instrument, but much more important is your personal achievement. If you are enjoying your lessons and are keen to practise, it doesn't matter if 'outward' progress is slow. In other words, one person's attainment may be much greater than another's, but if the achievement is your personal best, that's all that matters, and you should feel just as proud of it. If the whole thing becomes a chore and your enjoyment diminishes, it may be time to think again – but that should be a long way off, if it occurs at all.

A few people are born with what is known as perfect pitch. This means that they are able to give a sound its musical pitch name on hearing it played or sung. This can have advantages in certain areas of musical learning, but it can also have disadvantages. If you happen to have perfect pitch, it is likely you will show aptitude for music, but it is most certainly not a deciding factor when it comes to learning an instrument, so if you find pitching or holding a note difficult, don't allow that fact to discourage you from starting. By getting involved in some musical activity your sense of pitch will improve, and a good teacher should be able to help you nurture your aural perception and overcome this challenge.

Rhythm, pulse and beat are terms that are often used incorrectly by people when they speak about music, and it may be worth being sure you understand them at this preliminary stage. Most pieces of music have a pulse or beat, much like the pulse of a living creature. If we run around our pulse speeds up, and then gradually slows down as we rest and recover. Most pieces of music have a steady pulse, which may be at a fast tempo or a slower one. It is the pulse that we march to, or tap our feet to, not the rhythm. In many sorts of music the pulse is referred to as the beat. Rhythmic patterns overlay the pulse, and some learners find it easy to maintain a steady pulse and play differing rhythms against it. Others find this more difficult.

Again, this is not a reason to abandon the idea of learning, and a good teacher will be able to help you, as a learner, to get through any difficulties you may have. We say that some people seem to have a natural sense of rhythm if they find learning to play rhythms easy. You can check the difference between pulse and rhythm by simply taking a tune that you know – for example, 'Happy Birthday to You' – and 'tapping' the words with one hand and the pulse with the other. Try separate hands first and then hands together. If you want to make it a little more difficult, swap hands.

A similar situation applies with pitch. Some people are able to hear a note and sing it back confidently and accurately straightaway, whilst others find this very difficult, getting it right sometimes, but often being inconsistent. Once again, a good teacher will be able to help almost any learner overcome this difficulty. By taking part in a choir or choral group of any kind, you should find that singing will almost certainly help to improve your ability to identify and respond to pitch.

Reading music is something that most people absorb quite easily as part of learning to play their instrument. Most teachers include teaching learners how to read music as part of their instrumental tuition, and it is generally easier to learn music-reading this way, as part of the process of developing a 'symbol – sound – action' approach to music-making. In other words, seeing the note on the page, hearing the appropriate sound in your mind, and taking the action necessary to produce that sound. By associating the sound with the printed symbol, and as part of a specific hand or finger placement or movement, the brain absorbs the information more effectively through the process known as kinaesthetic learning. Being a confident and fluent music reader is developed over time, and by doing lots of sight reading, playing pieces that are new to you.

On some instruments, for example the piano, pressing a given key gives you a specific sound, so when reading music it is simply a matter of pressing the right key at the right time. The situation is similar on the clarinet and oboe. On other instruments, particularly members of the brass family, it is perfectly possible – and in fact essential – that pressing one valve can produce several notes with different pitches, so it is essential that the player can hear the sound they want before attempting to play it.

Playing music with other musicians also improves music-reading in general and sight-reading in particular, where the golden rule is to 'keep going', no matter how many wrong sounds you may produce. There are many publications that focus exclusively on sight-reading, and a number of 'apps' that can help overcome the challenge of becoming a more proficient music reader.

MUSIC THEORY

There is also the question of how important it is to learn some musical theory, away from your instrument. Although this can be a rather dry and dusty part of the learning process, there's no reason why it should be, and there is no doubt that it will help you to increase your fluency in reading and mastering all the intricacies of written or printed notation. Through understanding more about the form and context of musical compositions, especially those of Western classical tradition, you will find it easier to represent the composer's wishes in your performances of the music.

The theory of music is a part of musical study which you may have encountered already, and sadly, it may have a negative resonance for you. For a variety of reasons, the 'theory' of music has often been taught separately from the matter of making music itself. One of the contributory factors influencing this is the simple fact that it is perfectly possible to make music that is meaningful, communicative and interesting without needing, or being able, to notate your composition or articulate its form, structure and harmonic content. It is also perfectly possible to learn about notation and harmony without ever playing or hearing a note of music.

Music examinations, such as 'O' level in the middle of the last century, actually required the ability to notate without hearing live sounds, on the basis that developing your ability to hear the sounds you wished to notate, or your inner ear, was a vital component of being a musician. While this is true, it also seems much more pragmatic to enable the development of that aural perception through working with sound from the beginning, and gradually removing the sound source as you develop the skill of inner hearing. The situation was to some extent reinforced by the music exam boards, who have always published separate practical and theory graded exam syllabuses. The majority of tutor books ever published have included a page or two of musical rudiments, which usually show some basic elements of notation.

Musical literacy, the 'nuts and bolts' of getting musical sound on to music manuscript paper, is at the heart of the exam boards' early theory grades. Once those basics are understood, it is a question of studying the simple principles of harmony, which in the long term are of benefit to anyone learning to play a musical instrument or to sing, because they help you to understand the way sounds work together. Understanding this begins to unlock the door to effective communication in musical performance. Further study of harmony can provide a secure base for composition, which may start with compositions that are a pastiche of music from the baroque and classical eras, and then lead on to you writing freely in your own style as an independently minded composer. The approach to both practical and theoretical music is mostly very different today. There is a widely accepted belief that it works better to teach music-making and theory together, and the vast majority of music teachers teach music-reading through playing because it is easier to remember the notes on the stave if they are connected with how to produce the sound on your instrument. Taking a little time to spend a few moments in practical lessons on essential musical literacy benefits most learners, so is time well spent. This a far cry from the instruction found in one clarinet tutor book published at the end of the nineteenth century, which advises the student to 'commit to memory the fingering and use of the keys before attempting to produce the sound'. Incidentally, the book is still in print today.

The other key factor in the twenty-first century is the digitization of musical sound. This technical development has enabled us to do everything from storing our music collections on mp3 files to using auto-accompaniments with which to practise, and in many respects it could be argued that it has pushed the need for any understanding of musical theory way down the list of priorities for learners. It is now possible to make a four-track recording on your phone, or get help with writing lyrics, creating a melody, adding chords to your melody and notating the finished product – on your phone! Therefore it comes as no surprise that many young people learning an instrument attach less importance to learning musical theory than ever before.

Perhaps the most important point regarding this revolution in the growth of supporting materials for musicians at all stages of their development, is that it is akin to the rise of internet usage. In other words, the rise in the availability of information is not necessarily matched with a rise in knowledge and understanding.

As an adult learner, it will be your choice as to how much time and energy you give to learning some musical theory, and there is no suggestion that it should dominate your wish to make music with your voice or on an instrument, especially at the outset of your musical learning journey. Far from it. As time goes on and you become a more proficient performer of music, any time you choose to give to developing a better understanding of notation, composition, form, structure, history and the background associated with the music you are studying, will give you a deeper knowledge of music in context. It is this that will ultimately complement and enhance your natural abilities to perform music in a communicative and effective manner.

SINGING

Throughout this book the focus is on learning to play a musical instrument, but almost everyone has their own instrument to start with: their singing voice. Singing is one of the healthiest and most pleasurable musical activities you can engage in. Singing actually does you good because the very act of singing encourages the brain to release endorphins, and when this happens, you feel happier. Singing is fun! Singing in a well directed choir or group of any kind, can give immense satisfaction. This could be a very easy and economic starting point for anyone keen to take up music-making and as a precursor to starting an instrument, because the act of singing with others will help you to develop your aural skills, which are an essential part of all music-making.

Sadly, despite a number of excellent initiatives and a number of television programmes focused on singing, it is less common-place in many schools than it used to be. The desire to imitate the styles of vocalization heard in popular music means that many children never learn to sing properly, and some never develop the full vocal range with which they are born. If you plan to have, or have already started, instrumental lessons, you will benefit enormously from doing some singing, because it will help you to develop aural skills and perception. The best instrumentalists and singers listen carefully to the sounds they are making. They are acutely aware of imperfections in tone, timbre, pitch, dynamics and so on. It is often said that if you can sing it, you can play it!

There is an increasing number of opportunities for adults to sing. For example, many churches and religious groups have choirs and are usually keen to recruit new members, and local amateur dramatics groups often offer the opportunity to gain experience on stage through joining a chorus. Becoming a member of some sort of singing group is highly likely to be beneficial, whether it is a formally rehearsed choir tackling a more serious repertoire, or a less formally structured group. It may be a suitable stepping-stone to helping you to decide if you want to take a greater interest in music-making and move on to learning an instrument, if you still feel unsure about making the commitment.

JOINING A MUSIC ENSEMBLE

If you make a start with an orchestral or band instrument you will sooner or later elect, or be invited, to join a music ensemble for a rehearsal, and it may be worth thinking about a few points before you set off. It's worth checking, for example, if you are expected to bring your own music stand, and if you are, to make sure you feel confident putting it up and collapsing it afterwards. It may also be worth putting a discreet name tag on it so that it doesn't get swallowed up and mislaid after the rehearsal, if the group is a large one. If it is a small group in someone's house and you are playing a wood- or brasswind instrument, your hosts may be used to having players around. But if they are not familiar with hosting rehearsals, note, for example, the colour of the carpet, if there is one, as you could easily leave watermarks from your wood- or brasswind instrument, and take steps to protect the carpet. Another point is that if you find you're sharing a music stand with another player, one of you will be responsible for turning the pages, and that duty usually falls to the lower-ranked player, or is decided by agreement. These are all small points, but if you are feeling at all nervous, you want to do everything you can to keep stress levels at a minimum.

Once you have overcome any nervousness or apprehension you may have about joining an ensemble – and that will usually have disappeared by the second rehearsal – you will find that making music with others is one of the most satisfying things imaginable. It will really help your ears develop the ability to know how in tune your playing is, and will help you become sensitive as to how loud or quiet your playing is.

You may come across the film *Whiplash*: however, don't allow it to put you off starting to learn an instrument. It's a great film, but fortunately most, if not all, music teaching isn't quite as abrasive as the style portrayed in this film.

CHAPTER 3

Your Musical Experience to Date

Many people have a built-in fear of doing something musical, perhaps because they are afraid of the criticism they may receive. Curiously, when young children bring home some artwork from primary school we often celebrate their achievement, and the new masterpiece is ceremoniously hung on the wall or stuck on the fridge door. But when they bring home a violin and begin to coax a few none-too-appealing sounds from it, some adults are often much more critical of what they are trying to do.

This chapter explores the context in which music learning takes place, and where your experience of it to date has brought you.

TACKLING LACK OF CONFIDENCE

You may think you're not good enough to play a musical instrument, but for some people, tackling anything new brings with it a feeling of self-doubt. Others have sufficient self-confidence to believe in their ability to succeed. Perhaps your lack of confidence stems from some less-than-positive encounters with music while you were at school, or maybe your family saw it, or continues to see it, as a less-than-worthwhile pursuit. If, on the other hand, your hesitation comes from a fear that you won't have the necessary musical ability, then this is a different matter.

Let's consider negative experiences at school first. Here it is simply a question of saying to yourself that those days are in the past, and reminding yourself that you are now in a position to determine what happens to you. If you don't enjoy the learning experience, or you don't like the teacher, you can find another one. If the instrument doesn't feel quite right for you, you can try a different one. It's up to you to make the decisions and to trust your gut reaction and your feelings. And if you are worried about not having enough musical ability, you can put aside that concern straightaway. There are few, if any, individuals who are unable to play music, albeit at a simple level, and your enjoyment and satisfaction should come from what you can achieve, rather than bench-marked attainment. In other words, you may not pass a particular graded music exam, but if you are enjoying and benefiting from the experience and have done your best, that's all that matters.

MUSIC EXPERIENCED AT SCHOOL

As you will know from your own experience, and from the true stories of some adults (see Chapter 9), we have all had different encounters with music in the classroom when we were at school. Since the introduction of the National Curriculum in the UK, following the 1988 Education Reform Act, music has been a statutory subject in Key Stages one, two and three – which incidentally were also introduced in the Act. Important though this inclusion is, it has not been matched by a similar commitment to teacher training in music. Many primary school teachers, for whom music is just one of ten or more subject areas they are expected to cover, may have had as little as fifteen hours spent on the delivery of this subject during their entire training. So clearly, unless they already possess some significant musical skills, it is highly unlikely they will be particularly effective as music teachers.

For some people music was one of the highlights of their schooldays, whilst for others it was neither pleasurable nor memorable. That can make it even harder for some individuals, who have literally been 'scared off' from participating in any musical activity to risk going back to it. There is also a group of adults who had some instrumental lessons at school or out of school time and, for what is usually a variety of reasons, didn't derive much pleasure from their experience. It may help to explore some background musical issues to understand why your experience was not as good as perhaps it should have been.

WHAT IS CLASSICAL MUSIC?

Music from Western Europe and North America is often subdivided conversationally into four broad categories: popular, sometimes called rock'n'pop, classical, folk and jazz. The terms mean enough to most of us to give them some value. Of course, ask any enthusiast and they'll offer numerous subdivisions within these broad categories. It may be worth spending a moment just clarifying the bigger definitions while keeping in mind what the term 'music' meant at school. Before the introduction of CSEs in the 1960s, school music had a classical music bias, although this was being steadily eroded, and when CSE was replaced by GCSE in the mid-1980s, music of all genres and cultures was included in the curriculum.

As adults, when we think about popular music, we are mostly referring to music created and recorded since World War II, or the middle of the last century. The emphasis here is on the performance and/or recording of the music, because it is the performance of the music by the original artist that matters most. The notation of the music is of secondary importance. Some, or all of the sound is likely to be created using electronic instruments. Most of the pieces are short in length, and a large number are for dancing to. It is most likely that to learn to play popular music you will have a teacher who has performance experience in this genre and with whom you can identify.

A defining feature of pop music is the importance of the original performer, whereas in classical music it is the expected norm to enjoy performances of composers' works given by a number of individuals. The ownership of the music when in a classical style belongs more to the individual, and in that sense is more accessible to everyone who seeks to play, sing or perform it, while pop music belongs more to the individual(s) who made it famous.

Many electric guitarists are inspired to learn by hearing, and perhaps seeing, someone who is well known. Their sole ambition may be to imitate the sound they have heard, and so they practise and practise until eventually they achieve success with one particular piece. They then move on to the next piece, thus slowly and steadily consolidating their technique in a way which usually includes memorizing the pieces they are learning. If playing the electric guitar is your ambition, and this form of learning is one that appeals to you, there is no doubt that it will serve your needs well.

The term 'folk music' is applied to a wide range of music including traditional music, world music, and music that developed from the mid-twentieth-century revival of folk music. Traditional music centres on an aural tradition where a piece evolves over generations as it is passed on aurally from one generation to the next, or from one performer to another. It is music that, once written down, loses almost as much as it gains, and the credited 'composer' will often be anonymous. Several classical composers – such as the Englishman, Ralph Vaughan Williams, and the Australian, Percy Grainger – sought to collect and notate traditional folksongs at the beginning of the twentieth century. Perhaps the best known collector is Cecil Sharp, who founded the English Folk

Dance Society in 1911, which now has its home at Cecil Sharp House in London; the Vaughan Williams memorial library is also found here.

Jazz as a musical form has its origins in the southern states of North America in the closing years of the nineteenth century, and was created by black musicians. It invariably involves a significant amount of improvisation, even when notation is used. There are numerous subsets within the genre. If your interest is primarily in playing jazz, you could have in mind a woodwind or brass instrument, such as the clarinet, saxophone, trumpet or trombone, or something from a jazz rhythm section such as an electric bass, guitar, drums or piano. You could start learning any of these instruments with a teacher whose main focus is classical music and acquire the essential playing technique required to create and control the sound. The key difference is in developing fluency in improvisation, as some classically trained teachers/musicians will be reluctant to take this on.

A specialist jazz teacher will make sure that you include improvisation from the outset, so that you think more aurally about the music and the sounds you want to create, rather than perfecting the skill of playing as you read from written notation. It may be argued that all effective teachers should include work on improvisation as one of their teaching strategies, but this is not always the case, so you may need to explore this issue further during your initial conversations with your would-be teacher, if you really want to make jazz your priority as a learner.

When we speak of classical music we usually use the term to describe any form of composition that is based on notation and written primarily for listening to, as distinct from providing an accompaniment to dancing or marching. The term is widely applied to music composed between about 1100 and the present day. Within that large time-frame, the classical period itself is of modest proportions. It is exemplified by the works of Haydn and Mozart, and extends only from the late eighteenth century through to about 1830. One way of defining classical music is to emphasize, as did the great conductor, Leonard Bernstein, the fact that the composer's notation is precisely what he or she wanted to hear being played. A conductor or the performers may vary the way the notation is interpreted, but the notation itself is of paramount importance. This is much less true of folk music, pop or jazz.

The more 'classical' approach to learning and teaching is adopted by most teachers of Western classical instruments, particularly for players who expect to spend time in bands, ensembles and orchestras. Here there is an emphasis on the teaching of reading music, which goes hand in hand with the development and acquisition of instrumental technique. All these teaching and learning strategies are equally valid.

Children, especially younger ones, are usually willing to be guided by their teacher, and so their musical diet, and to some extent their preferences, will often be strongly influenced by him or her. As an adult learner you should expect to have a greater say in the music that will be used to help you develop skills, alongside pieces or studies that you are learning and playing, because you have chosen them. This may be something to discuss with a prospective teacher at a preliminary interview or during your first lesson. For example, focusing exclusively on an examination syllabus may not be in your best interests unless that is particularly what you want to do, and in several of the true stories related in this book you'll find reference to the negative aspects of learning from such a syllabus, rather than learning from a curriculum constructed for the benefit of you, the individual learner.

Effective teachers will have developed their own teaching curriculum and should be able to articulate their personalized plans for each learner's musical development. For many learners, playing as part of an ensemble will be an essential component of the learning process. The ensemble could be an orchestra, a string group, a wind group, a windband, a brass band, a jazz band, a percussion group, a big band, a clarinet choir, a flute ensemble, a string quartet, a brass quintet, a saxophone quartet, a guitar group, a rock group, or just about any combination of instrumentalists getting together to make music.

Most people learning to play an instrument find that a mix of individual or small group tuition, combined with the opportunity to play in a larger group each week, is the most effective way of developing their instrumental technique securely, alongside their musical understanding and musicianship. The only area of sensitivity may be that of finding yourself playing next to someone a good deal younger than you are. If this is a problem for you, then simply bide your time until you are a little more secure on your instrument, or seek out a different ensemble to join.

Part of the process of learning to play a musical instrument is learning to understand a variety of compositional and performance styles. For most people, the idea of developing a broader understanding which provides a secure basis for moving to a more in-depth study later on, is both acceptable and the most desirable.

MUSIC EXAMS, COMPETITIONS AND FESTIVALS

Graded music examinations have been around for well over one hundred years. Several different independent exam boards provide them, and the format usually involves the preparation of several pieces chosen from the board's exam syllabus, along with supporting tests, which are performed to an examiner who awards marks and writes comments. After processing by the exam board, the results are forwarded to the teacher and hence to the student and parents. A certificate is issued to successful candidates, and a mark sheet to all candidates.

For many learners exams can be highly motivational: they create the desire to outstrip peers, and may help to encourage daily practice. Most graded music exams can be taken by learners of any age, and although there are usually in the region of eight grades, it is rarely a requirement of the exam board that all grades must be taken, or taken in any particular sequence. Used selectively by an effective teacher, graded exams provide a milestone of attainment for students and a measurement of personal achievement to date.

Where exams create a problem is when teachers respond to the exam syllabus by adopting it as a ready-made curriculum. This style of 'teaching to the test' can result in poorly motivated students who are perhaps good at passing exams, but are not motivated to succeed as musicians. It seems that many people who had music exam success at school and were very active music makers, found no difficulty in leaving their music-making behind when they left school. That is not to say that there is a correlation between the two, but it is important for you to reflect on your own feelings if you took music exams at school, or would like to take music exams as an adult learner.

Competitions and festivals can work in a similar way to exams as either motivators or de-motivators for learners. The key difference between an exam and a festival or competition is that the exam is a private matter between candidate and examiner, whereas a competition or festival usually takes place in public and the adjudication is commonly given verbally in public, followed by the distribution of written comments to participants and the celebratory award of a trophy of some sort. Some learners may find this highly motivational, while others would experience it as a discouraging and even humiliating experience. It would be as well to attend as a member of the audience before submitting an entry form for such a competition.

Music is set apart from other subjects by its use of graded exams, and it is worth spending a few extra moments thinking about these exams and the way they impact on both teaching and learning. The two largest music exam boards in the UK are the Associated Board of the Royal Schools of Music (ABRSM) and Trinity College London (TCL). Both boards have their origins in late Victorian England, TCL having been founded in 1877 and ABRSM in 1889. There are also a number of smaller music exam boards. ABRSM and TCL were created in part to support instrumental teachers who sought to prepare candidates for auditions to enter certain music conservatoires, particularly the Royal College of Music, the Royal Academy of Music and Trinity College of Music. At the outset the eight grades that are used today were not available, but over time, both exam boards moved to the eight-grade structure, with an additional preparatory or initial exam preceding Grade 1. Both boards now publish exam syllabuses that contain specified pieces chosen for each grade, which are set alongside a series of supporting tests including aural, scales and sight-reading.

Many teachers adopt these exam syllabuses as a form of ready-made curriculum, simply preparing candidates for each grade in turn. While this enables learners to achieve success in terms of the number of passes they achieve and certificates they obtain, in musical terms it constitutes a rather incomplete learning diet, even when linked to the eight grades of theory that each board also offers. The graded exams of both boards can be taken as and when desired, and there is no requirement to pass one exam before taking the next one. In other words, it is perfectly possible to start the exam ladder at grade two or three, or even higher. Graded exams are available from the various music exam boards for the Western classical tradition, for jazz, rock and pop, traditional music and Indian classical music.

On the plus side, exams can be a powerful source of motivation for learners, and may, for children at school, hold the key to being able to audition for a particular group within the school, or at local, county, regional or national level. For some adult learners, graded music exams can provide a stimulus to achievement, and constitute an easy measure of success by which they can compare their progress with that of their own children or grandchildren. For others, the fear of a one-to-one encounter with an examiner may have a significantly negative impact on the learning experience, perhaps even enough to cause them to cease having lessons.

Any experienced teacher who enters students regularly for graded music exams should be able to give you a reliable indication as to whether you would pass or fail at a particular grade, and whether your performance would earn you a 'pass, merit or distinction' – so you might feel that you don't have to bother with the exam itself. Either way, it's important to determine from the outset whether your teacher is flexible in their approach to the use of exams and is able to accommodate your preferences, especially as your view may change once you have started to make progress. It is also worth noting that as an adult learner you can enter yourself for a graded music exam, so if you choose to learn without the support of a teacher, you are in no way barred from the opportunity to take graded exams.

A TYPICAL INSTRUMENTAL LESSON TODAY

Let's take a look at an instrumental music lesson today. There is really no such thing as a typical lesson, because every teacher will approach their work differently, but we can follow some common patterns. An enjoyable and effective instrumental lesson will usually include a variety of activities suited to the age, ability and needs of the learner. Learning to play music on an instrument involves multi-tasking, so the learner needs to be able to do the following: listen to themselves and sometimes other players too; make the sounds; control the sounds; pay attention to the pulse, rhythm, dynamics and phrasing of the music; and probably read the music as well.

If you've learned to drive a car you may recall that you experienced a certain amount of fear and trepidation in your first few driving lessons, when there seemed to be an enormous number of things to do at once: changing gear, using the indicators, watching the traffic, checking your mirror and so on. However, most people master the skill of doing all these things, and soon, driving a car becomes something that we do almost automatically. You may find that starting to learn an instrument is in some respects similar, so don't let any worries about initial difficulties put you off.

Most teachers develop their own routine for lessons, and there is more than one way of giving an effective lesson. Many teachers begin with some musical warm-up activities, and go on to include some work with and without musical notation – this might include scales, aural development, studies and pieces. For some instruments, such as trumpet or clarinet or violin, the warm-ups are helping you to build stamina; for others, such as the piano, this is less important. A typical lesson for a beginner may last for thirty minutes, although some brass teachers may opt for a little less at the outset. A lot can be covered in that time, and while an adult may feel able to concentrate for longer, it is actually doubtful that more would necessarily be accomplished or achieved.

A style of teaching that may be less effective is where the teacher always starts at the beginning of the piece and will only allow you, as a learner, to move forwards when everything you have played is completely correct. This may mean that a whole lesson is spent on just a bar or two of music, and this can be very frustrating for some learners. Others, however, may like this very thorough and rigorous approach. A more creative approach could involve your teacher identifying the areas that you, as the learner, are likely to find challenging as an individual, and making up some exercises to help you overcome those difficulties before you have even seen the notation of the piece you are about to learn. By working in this way you are less intimidated by the notation, and more focus is placed on your interpretation of the music and the composer's wishes.

Western classical music played by orchestras and bands usually involves reading music. It is quite difficult, and perhaps less useful, to learn to read musical notation in abstract, without the benefit of kinaesthetic learning. This is what happens when, for example, you hold your instrument. It becomes easier to remember that pressing down a particular finger produces a given sound, which on music manuscript looks 'like this'. The absence of kinaesthesia partly explains why some singers are less good at reading a new piece from musical notation, whereas orchestral and band players may develop this skill to very high levels. In certain genres, music is learnt off by heart. For example, much pop music and traditional music is often performed without recourse to any written notation, and players usually learn the music aurally – by listening and imitating, and practising repeatedly until they've got it right. Few classical teachers work this way, although some will teach beginners to play 'by rote'. The majority will teach, and expect learners to develop fluency in, reading musical notation.

The most effective teachers will include some work involving improvisation – playing without written music – in their lessons. This does not mean having to play jazz, but simply implies making up a short passage from notes suggested by the teacher. You may be asked to play them quietly or loudly, short or long, in order to gain more familiarity with fingering or bowing, and your instrument in general. Some teachers may include jazz. Improvisation helps to develop musical thinking skills and aural perception.

Some learners have a natural aptitude for music, and quickly pick up an understanding of the various elements of music as they gain mastery of their chosen instrument. Some may make rapid progress, and these may also tire more quickly of their learning and look for something new to do. Learners who find the combination of musical actions necessary to play a piece difficult to master may need to take more time to assimilate skills, but with the right sort of teacher they can still prosper – they will simply do so more slowly. Acquiring skills associated with the mastery of any given instrument is simply a question of time, dedication and hard work, and there are few, if any, successful performers who haven't spent hours practising.

Most instruments can be taught in a group teaching and learning situation, and many children feel more comfortable learning in this way, especially in the early stages. As an adult learner you are less likely to find yourself in this situation, but if the idea appeals to you it may be worth exploring, and you may feel more comfortable sharing your lessons with a friend or colleague. Some teachers specialize in this way of teaching, while others concentrate on providing one-to-one tuition: basically there is no right or wrong way of teaching someone to play a musical instrument. Group tuition may be a little cheaper, and for some learners may provide a more secure atmosphere. There are many other good reasons for learning and teaching in groups, and these are explored more fully in the section 'Individual or Group Lessons?' in Chapter 4.

Learning is not a smooth curve for most people. There will be plateaux when things don't seem to improve, and again both learner and teacher should expect this and allow for it. Learning and mastering new skills as a player takes time, and it also takes time for these skills to be assimilated and consolidated – hence the absence of a smooth learning curve for the majority.

The physical environment in which the lesson takes place will be more important for some learners than others. If the lesson takes place at the teacher's home, you should check that you feel comfortable with the room in which the teaching takes place, and perhaps ask questions of the teacher about their experience of working there. In the UK there is no regulation of private teaching, which means it is up to the learner to make any checks they feel are necessary themselves.

Overall there can be little doubt that the most effective lesson will have practical music-making at the heart of it. Lessons where 'teacher talk' predominates are likely to be less successful, although there will always be occasions when lesson content, if taken in isolation, may seem unbalanced.

MUSIC SERVICES (UK)

In the UK, most local authorities (LA) have a Music Service, which provides instrumental, vocal and other forms of musical tuition to schools. The Music Service provides ready access, for children at maintained schools, to instrumental lessons. Most Music Services make a termly charge for tuition, which varies according to the number of children being taught in a group. Independently funded schools make their own arrangements for instrumental teachers to visit their schools, and parents are usually billed by the school for a term's tuition.

In addition to the provision of one-to-one, or small group tuition, most LA Music Services run evening or Saturday morning music centres, and these provide opportunities for children to join ensembles of a level appropriate to their ability and experience. Such ensembles are an invaluable addition to anything that most schools can provide, and most instrumental teachers would agree that playing in an ensemble helps to motivate learners, to improve their standards, and enhance their awareness of many musical matters.

Music Services are included in this book for adult music learners for two main reasons: first, their role in music education since the middle of the last century is highly significant; and second, you may find that your local Music Service or music centre welcomes adults to join their music workshops, groups or ensembles – and in any event, your LA Music Service, as part of a music hub, can usually be a valuable source of information about music teaching and music-making in your locality.

CHAPTER 4

Tutors, Teachers

Instrumental and vocal teaching is often referred to as 'music tuition'. However, it is difficult, if not impossible, to provide an absolutely clear definition of the terms 'teaching' and 'tuition' and to draw a clear distinction between them, as in both contexts there can be one-to-one or group work. One commonly found difference is that tuition is often referred to as 'taking place at home', and arises as a direct result of the learner making an arrangement with the tutor, whereas teaching often takes place in a more formal setting. Even so, it's not completely clear, because many people will refer to their piano teacher as the person from whom they had lessons. Throughout this book the terms are used interchangeably.

Here are some questions to start you thinking about what kind of learner you are:

- Do you prefer to have individual attention when learning something new, or would you rather be part of a group?
- Do you tend to judge people more by their appearance, their words or their actions?
- Do you think you would prefer a male or a female teacher?
- Are you likely to make a strong commitment to learning and stick to it?

PRIVATE TEACHERS

The term 'private teacher' is used in the UK to describe a self-employed music teacher. The majority teach in their own homes, but some will travel to you and teach you in your home, or perhaps at your workplace, if surroundings permit. When engaging a private teacher it is wise to arrange a preliminary or introductory lesson, and many teachers are willing to, or may insist on, doing this. Such a lesson will allow you to see that an appropriate room is being used, especially if the teaching takes place in a private dwelling house. In addition to the size of the room, you may want to think about its layout and take a look at the equipment the teacher has available, and how much use they make of their range of resources –

for example piano, music stand, computer, software, sound system, and so on. It is also interesting to see if your would-be teacher actually demonstrates on their instrument. There are two schools of thought about this: one maintains that demonstration is essential and integral to every lesson; the other says that the teacher's role is to explain and teach, rather than play during a student's lesson. My preference is for the former approach where the teacher demonstrates, but both strategies can work well. All of this will give you an indication, but no more, of your teacher's approach to their work. The size of the room also gives you some idea of whether your teacher will need to sit or stand very close to you as the lesson proceeds.

The private music teacher has to cover a lot of educational ground, which might include the following: developing their own knowledge of materials and repertoire for students at different stages of their musical development; planning individual lessons and overall schemes of work for their students; teaching individual and/or group lessons; arranging lesson schedules, collecting fees and entering students for examinations; developing networks and establishing collaborations with others working in music education; supporting students in their use of music technology; ensuring that they adhere to health and safety standards, are adequately insured, and work in line with child protection legislation; managing the administrative tasks associated with running a small business, including tax and finance issues; and marketing their teaching practice.

It may therefore be useful to ascertain how much time your teacher spends on teaching privately, especially if they have adopted or assumed the label of private teacher. Some may have a full-time job in another field and just fit in some private teaching during the evenings or at weekends to supplement their earnings, and some may be part-time or full-time employees of a school or Music Service.

You may also care to find out whether the private teacher takes steps to keep themselves up to date in matters of teaching and learning through attendance at, and participation in, continuing professional development courses. You could find out if they are members of one of the professional organizations, for example the Incorporated Society of Musicians (ISM) or Musicians' Union (MU) in the UK. They may also be a member of a subject-specific organization, such as the European String Teachers' Association (ESTA). Although being a member of such an organization doesn't necessarily provide any specific guarantee as to the quality of their teaching, it does indicate that your teacher is interested in maintaining a profile within the instrumental music-teaching profession and community, and is aware of the importance of continuing professional development. A list of music associations, organizations and professional bodies can be found at the end of this book. The vast majority of private music teachers are hard-working, enthusiastic musicians and teachers. Many give outstanding service for quite modest fees, often going the extra mile when additional preparation is needed for a particular musical event, be it a concert, exam or festival. It is always interesting to know if a private teacher is active as a performing musician, which is something one would reasonably expect – although some private teachers may have strong and valid reasons for no longer wishing to perform in public.

TEACHER/TUTOR QUALIFICATIONS

You might ask if it matters what qualifications your teacher or tutor has – and the short answer is that it doesn't. You may feel that you value experience over qualifications, or you may prefer youthful enthusiasm over experience. The single most important thing is that you feel able to learn from the way your teacher teaches, but it may be worth spending a few moments exploring the different and most commonly found forms of qualification, and the routes by which they are acquired.

Music teachers may be employed by local authorities or schools to work as classroom teachers, or by Music Services where their work is principally focused on small group teaching. Alternatively they may be 'private' teachers who provide tuition in their own homes. The crucial difference is that in the UK, to teach in the classroom teachers need to have an undergraduate degree and teaching qualification, but the requirements for instrumental teachers have always been slightly different because instrumental tuition, in the form provided by LA Music Services, is not a part of the statutory curriculum. Instrumental teaching was traditionally based on one-to-one or small group teaching, which meant that teachers did not have to have 'qualified teacher status' (QTS).

At the beginning of the twentieth century, the training of classroom teachers became established as a form of higher education, enabling the new local education authorities (LEAs) to make secondary schools available for the training of pupil teachers. It was simultaneously recognized that intending teachers should receive a complete course of education in secondary schools. The routes into teaching have varied considerably over the past hundred years or more, but from 1992, QTS was a requirement for all class teachers until a change was made by government in 2014. As Music Services developed after World War II, instrumental music teachers who worked for them did not need a classroom teaching qualification. For many years the qualification of choice for instrumental and singing teachers working privately was a music diploma, and diplomas came in two broad categories, performing and teaching. Furthermore it was perfectly possible to be awarded a teaching diploma having done very little, or no teaching at all. In recent times, however, the landscape of qualifications has changed significantly – for example, the LRAM and ARCM teaching diplomas made available by the Royal Academy of Music and the Royal College of Music in London can now no longer be taken as external examinations. In 2013 a new qualification, the Certificate for Music Educators (level 4) was launched, and this is proving attractive both to new entrants to the music education profession and to many well established teachers, as it covers aspects of the work such as child protection, inclusivity and equal opportunities, which have only come sharply into focus in recent years.

It was the view of many people that in order to learn to play music you needed to learn from someone who had attained, and perhaps maintained, high standards as a performing musician. It is probably also true to say that the number of children learning in school remained at around 10 per cent of the school population during this period, although that figure does not account for the number of children learning privately out of school hours, which includes the majority of piano pupils. But since the end of the twentieth century and into the twenty-first century there has been a move to a different way of thinking, and now, for the most part we no longer test children for musical aptitude and then give lessons only to those who show promise or potential, but instead, the more inclusive view is taken that everyone who wishes to try learning a musical instrument should have the opportunity to do so.

It may be said that music teachers with a broader view teach music through the instrument, rather than merely focusing on the technique necessary to play music on that instrument. An effective teacher teaches technical skills, musicianship, music reading, care of the instrument, musical theory, some music history, music of different genres, development of aural perception, playing music as part of an ensemble, and a host of other skills.

INDIVIDUAL OR GROUP LESSONS?

Until recently the expected answer to this question would be: 'If you can afford it and want to make good progress, you must have individual tuition.' There are many teachers who would subscribe to this point of view, but an equally large number who would now recommend group lessons, particularly for beginners.

There are many reasons for this change of thinking, and it is worth exploring just a few of those that relate to the way children are taught and how they learn most effectively. First, children are commonly taught in groups in their other school lessons, particularly in primary schools, and as a teaching strategy this is now common in the secondary years as well; second, peer group learning has been shown to be effective; third, we live in a time when one-to-one work with children is less acceptable as a general rule. Fourth, group teaching is often more cost effective from the delivery point of view; and fifth, group instrumental learning means that ensemble music-making is possible from the outset. Thinking back to your own school days, who was your first choice for advice when you were stuck with some work in the classroom? Did you ask your class teacher, or the person sitting next to you? It is often a school-mate, who can put things in simple and direct terms, and whose explanation can be most helpful.

That said, there may not be a choice between group and individual lessons, especially for an adult, and this may again occur for a number of reasons. First, it may not be possible to teach that particular instrument to a group in the smaller space likely to be available in a private house – a 'cello, for example, requires quite a lot of space, and there is rarely more than one piano in a room. Also, learners of instruments such as the French horn or oboe may be in short supply. From an adult learner's point of view it may simply be interesting to see if all the options available have been considered, or whether the teaching context is dictated by the attitude of the teacher, rather than by the most effective teaching strategy that could be deployed.

Whole class instrumental and vocal teaching in recent years has demonstrated that large-scale group learning is effective, and that learners can acquire musical skills on an instrument when taught in a group of as many as thirty learners. The brass band movement reflects this sentiment, and has operated in this way for many years.

As an adult learner you may not have access to this sort of framework for learning the instrument you have chosen, but if you have children, or grandchildren, of primary school age it may be possible for you to join their weekly instrumental lesson, and this is definitely worth considering, if logistics permit. And as mentioned above, the brass band is another area of music learning which is ensemble based. Many bands have a junior or training band that welcomes adult learners, and there is a strong tradition of working in this way for these ensembles. This could definitely be worth exploring in your locality if a brass instrument is the one you choose, and this approach is exemplified in one of the learning stories in Chapter 9.

BETWEEN LESSONS

To make progress with the learning of any musical instrument, whether as an individual or as part of a group, practice is essential. The old adage of 'little and often' is apposite as far as music is concerned – though if you have just acquired a drum kit or electric guitar, your neighbours may feel differently! As a learner you may find that, as with most things, you benefit from a regular routine for your practice. For a beginner on trumpet or oboe, ten minutes of focused practice every day will be highly beneficial and probably enough. Practising most days, rather than just on some days, is important, especially at the outset when you need to consolidate and assimilate a number of essential technical points usually connected with posture and sound production, and this applies to the singing voice and to all instruments.

Some instruments are physically a little less demanding, and your teacher will advise you as to the amount of time you could profitably spend playing each day. If you can establish a routine, it should be easy to extend it gradually to twenty or thirty minutes each day, or if appropriate and you have the time available, to several separate twenty- to thirty-minute sessions each day.

When choosing an instrument it is important to think about where it will be stored, and where and when it will be practised. Standing or sitting on a proper upright chair, rather than sitting on a sofa, will produce the best results. If notation is involved, a music stand should be used whenever possible, to help you develop a good playing posture. It is much easier to set out with the right habits from day one than trying to correct things after a few weeks or months of learning.

Some teachers will encourage learners to use a range of technology to support their learning – for example, listening to musical examples from a range of sound and visual sources. There is now a wide range of software designed to help learners, including programs to help develop aural skills and programs to help with the 'theory' of music. It may be helpful here to clarify the term 'theory': at its simplest level, this means acquiring knowledge and understanding of musical notation, and progresses to include a knowledge and understanding of harmony and composition. Many teachers now use software that provides an accompaniment or backing to a piece of music. Unlike earlier versions of recorded accompaniments, these accompanying tracks can be played at differing speeds whilst maintaining pitch, and can be played at differing pitches with the player's choice of tempo. More significantly, they can 'follow' the player, allowing you to slow down for more difficult passages.

Last but not least, the other thing that should happen between lessons is that your teacher will spend a little time thinking about, and preparing for your next lessons – in other words, being a pro-active teacher rather than simply reacting to the way you play in your next lesson. This is discussed more fully in Chapter 5.

PRACTISING

There are no short cuts to the overall process of learning to play a musical instrument. The difference between success and failure depends on many factors, the most important of which is practice. Many adults look back on their experiences of learning to play and remember, with dread, being made to practise. Learning to enjoy practice time depends on effective teaching, a well motivated learner, and a suitable and perhaps supportive environment.

Most people find that they benefit from making practice time part of a routine, and you may like to set aside a suitable time each day, and if you have a choice, a suitable place for this important homework to be done. Many adults are highly enthusiastic about practising because, after all, they have chosen to learn the instrument and really want to be successful.

Little and often is the best for beginners of all ages, when the repetition of physical actions enables kinaesthetic learning to take place naturally. Repetition of a particular movement or action enables it to be stored in muscle memory. If it isn't going right, it is best to stop and come back to it later, as frustration through not being able to do something hinders progress. Recording yourself practising, and spending a few minutes listening to and watching the results, is a really helpful way of self-appraising your work. It can enable you to put something right quickly, and you may find that something your teacher has said to you in a lesson is echoing in your mind as you watch or listen.

TEACHING YOURSELF

A question you might ask is, do I really need a teacher, or can I teach myself?

A quick internet search will reveal any number of websites providing tuition and advice on playing any musical instrument. Some offer free tuition, while others provide a free introduction followed by some form of subscription-based service. There is no doubt that many sites give easy access to high quality tuition and it is perfectly possible to learn in this way, but difficulties may arise when the instrument you have chosen to learn presents a greater challenge in terms of making the sound. Creating a sound on the piano is initially a straightforward process of pressing the key down and releasing it, which poses few if any problems for most beginners, but creating a sound on a brass instrument, flute or oboe, is potentially more difficult. It is possible to follow instruction given via a website, but any difficulties you encounter will almost certainly be overcome more easily if a teacher is present in the room with you.

One approach that can overcome this is a real-time internet-based lesson, for example using a service such as Skype. This form of video conference-styled teaching has been used to excellent effect by some UK Music Services working in rural areas, where the costs in terms of time and fuel for a teacher to visit schools is simply prohibitive. You may find a teacher who is able to work with you in this way if travelling to lessons is difficult for you. You may also wish to find out if they have experience of working in this way. Perhaps you could talk to one of their other students to help you decide if this is going to be right for you. Clearly, if you intend to 'invite someone into your home' via a webcam, caution will be needed. In short, there are huge benefits to having a real, live teacher, rather than relying on technology.

TUTORS: BOOKS AND METHODS

For as long as people have wanted to learn to play a musical instrument there have been 'instruction manuals' of all kinds produced to help them. They proliferated in Victorian times in the UK, when lithographic colour printing advanced, and enjoyed a period of growth as American music education developed the band method in the early twentieth century. In the USA there was further growth during World War II when the Music Educators National Convention (MENC) took the initiative to promote 'American Unity Through Music', which encouraged music educators to promote community spirit through singing, sharing musical materials, and instrumental work, all of which prepared student musicians for careers in the armed forces.

There is no doubt that a tutor or method book really supports learning for beginners because it provides a range of simple but progressively more difficult melodies to play, and usually addresses technical issues associated with the particular instrument. Such books may also provide some form of theory tuition, and opportunities for two- or three-part playing for melody instruments. In conjunction with a good teacher, such texts can be highly supportive. Where they are less than successful the teacher slavishly follows the content of the book, as this may result in too much time being spent on a particular technical aspect, or – and more commonly – too little time being spent on something that would have benefited from some personalized work, catering for the needs of the individual more effectively.

Most teachers will choose the book they would prefer to use, based on their experience, rather than leaving it to you as the learner, but don't be afraid to express an opinion on the matter. Sadly, the majority of texts are published with the needs of children and young people in mind, and few take a more adult view. That is why it is vital for your teacher to feel confident in bypassing some of the activities that a book may suggest, and either substituting or adding their own complementary work. An effective teacher should have no hesitation, for example, in composing their own pieces to suit your needs as a learner.

CHAPTER 5

Learning and Teaching

The ways in which teachers teach and learners learn have involved huge amounts of research in the past fifty years. In Victorian times, children in school were expected to sit still and quietly while the teacher explained things and set them exercises to complete. Current thinking is very different from this, and is focused on teachers being proactive in finding strategies to engage learners and help them understand through group interaction, question and answer, personalized learning and practical activity. Today, teachers aim to personalize or individualize teaching so that it will work best for each individual learner, reflecting that individual's needs.

Learning can take place with or without a teacher. In order to learn, learners usually need a motivation or stimulus. They may be motivated by observing their peers achieve something; by a reward of some kind, such as a treat, or cash; because they are forced or coerced into doing something; or from within themselves, because they really want to be able to do it! This last form of motivation – the intrinsic way – is the most powerful, though often with children it is the most elusive to sustain. Part of the process of growing up is discovering new things, being drawn to them, and then, just as suddenly, leaving them for the next new thing – and in terms of learning an instrument, this isn't very helpful! Part of the job of the teacher, supported by the parents where children are involved as learners, is to maintain motivation, particularly through these more difficult times.

Effective learning is characterized by perseverance, independence and skill acquisition. Progress, when learning a musical instrument, is not linear, and you don't just move forwards inexorably day by day – sometimes learners plateau, and sometimes they appear to get worse. Learning a new skill requires time for assimilation and consolidation, and learning to play a musical instrument involves the acquisition of fine motor skills and understanding the concepts of harmony, phrasing, dynamics, tone, intonation and timbre, and all of this along with reading music, listening and, in many instances, learning to co-operate with others.

Teaching encompasses a range of activity extending from encounter through teaching to instruction, and these areas may be explained as follows: first, instruction takes place when there is a clear, well defined outcome for the learner. The teacher or instructor doesn't look for any alternative outcome, but has one in mind from the outset, and the learner succeeds by adopting the instruction and carrying out any necessary activity. The sign on the door says 'Push', or 'Push to open', and it is an unequivocal instruction with no room for negotiation.

At the other end of the spectrum is encounter, which occurs when the learner is placed in the environment of something which they then 'tune into'. Teaching sits somewhere in the middle, and is characterized by the teacher allowing, and indeed encouraging, the possibility of different outcomes. If you think of a driving instructor, their tuition provides a great deal of information and instruction to enable you to acquire the skills you need to drive a car. Here, the emphasis is on non-negotiable instruction, and there isn't much room, if any, regarding how to do things. Teaching, by contrast, provides plenty of room for manoeuvre for both learner and teacher.

In the past in instrumental teaching, there has often been a greater focus on instruction in the early stages of learning, an emphasis on the right and wrong ways of doing things, and encounter is largely overlooked by some teachers, other than in certain contexts. It is in the world of popular music and, quite separately, in the world of brass band music, that encounter predominates. Here, learners get to know the music by listening to it, of their own choice. Then in the brass band world they have the opportunity to join in, actually playing an instrument but with minimal instruction.

In popular music, learners encounter the music, then imitate the sounds they have heard. They often work for a long time on mastering one particular piece, before moving on and starting the process over again with another piece. This way, they accumulate the technical skills that are required to play particular pieces, rather than studying pieces and engaging with technical exercises, such as scales, to improve mastery, as happens in 'classical' music learning.

Both methods work. When learning classical music there is an emphasis on reading notation, whereas in other musical styles the emphasis is more on memorizing and knowing a piece very well aurally.

Teaching, rather than instruction, usually dominates classroom work, and allows learners to follow their own ideas, so they learn by doing and experimenting. Teachers teach, facilitate and enable, creating opportunities for learners to learn, and their skill lies in knowing what to do next and in which direction to steer the learners so their motivation is maintained. These skills are encompassed in careful planning to ensure that all relevant material is covered, and the needs of the individual learner are met.

Instrumental tuition is sometimes over-dominated by instruction, which at one extreme may be brusque and ill-informed. This is usually found in reactive teaching, where the teacher reacts to the learner's musical mistakes. It is very easy for a teacher to work in this way because the vast majority of students will provide plenty of mistakes that the teacher can pick up on and perhaps correct. There is also the risk of a student simply copying the way the teacher chooses to play or perform a piece or passage of music. While there is great value in listening to, and copying performance characteristics, it is really important, as a learner, to be able to make your own musical decisions as you gain more confidence.

A better option is pro-active teaching, where the teacher spends time preparing the lesson and is able to anticipate the areas that learners will find difficult, and seek ways of enabling them to develop and acquire the necessary skills so as to avoid future mistakes occurring. Weak teaching, in any context, fails to recognize the constantly varying needs of different learners. It blames the learner when learning falters. In an ideal world, teachers will use a blend of all three strategies: encounter, teaching and instruction.

Up to about the middle of the last century, class teaching was little changed from Victorian times. Classes often contained thirty to forty or more pupils who were seated at desks and only expected to speak when invited to. Rote learning underpinned a lot of teaching: memorizing texts, chanting tables and so on. Whilst this may have a place in learning, it is only part of the process. From the 1960s onwards there has been huge change driven by a greater understanding of the learning process. We now talk about visual, auditory and kinaesthetic learning; we know that group working and collaboration are helpful; we distinguish more clearly between skills, knowledge and understanding. We place different values on the skills needed to access information and the abilities to develop deep understanding of a particular subject or topic. Shallow learning in music amounts to the ability to play the notes correctly, while deep learning means the ability to play the music in a communicative and engaging way.

In the world of instrumental teaching, many individuals have taken these ideas on board and adapted their approach to enable a broader range of students to achieve success, although it is probably true that instrumental music teaching has been slower to change than teaching in many other subjects. Perhaps this has something to do with the fact that much of the music we play, and the instruments we play it on, have been around, little changed, for a very long time. Whatever the reasons, it is vitally important that, when choosing your teacher, you find someone whose personality and way of teaching you can relate to, so that you can work together effectively and produce the outcomes you want.

PERFORMERS AND TEACHERS

Looking back over the past few hundred years of musical history in Europe, we see a long line of composer-performers, most of whom also did some teaching. The term 'virtuoso' is often applied to performers, and from the late eighteenth century the term started to be used to describe the musician, instrumentalist or vocalist who pursued a career as a soloist. As playing technique developed, composers rose to the challenge, writing more technically challenging pieces, and as composers and performers demanded more, the challenge was similarly taken up by instrument makers who wanted to ensure that their instruments would rise to the demands being placed upon them by virtuoso performers. This is clear in the music of the great nineteenth-century piano virtuoso and composer Liszt, for example, and coincides with the rise of the public concert hall and increased access to live performances for all.

As a beginner instrumentalist you may be wondering what this has to do with you, but it is the emphasis on technical prowess and accomplishment that in some respects has put a barrier between aspiring music learners and teachers, encouraging some teachers only to take on pupils who would be likely to succeed and do well. In our current, more inclusive approach to learning across the board, we now recognize that anyone who is interested in learning music should be encouraged to do so, regardless of whether they appear to have much, or little potential. We now perceive that taking part is more important and beneficial to the learner than whether they are able to achieve particularly high standards.

Musician and music educator Paul Harris has recently published a book which interestingly is called *The Virtuoso Teacher*, in which he talks about the skills that are needed by an effective teacher, and the importance which should be attached to learning with such a teacher. It reminds us that being a virtuoso performer in any musical context doesn't automatically mean that you will be a virtuoso teacher, and perhaps explains why some would-be music learners have been put off by their encounters with music and music-making. Your teacher needs to be patient and understanding, and to possess a range of strategies to enable you to learn – a veritable virtuoso teacher.

PREFERRED LEARNING STYLE

All learners, whatever their age, have a preferred learning style, although some will be more acutely aware of this than others. Many learners are either unaware of their preference or are unable to articulate it, or access it. There are numerous tests that you could take to help you determine your favoured approach, and an internet search may enable you to satisfy, to some extent, your curiosity about this. A good teacher will identify your preferred learning style through engaging with you, and will work to your strengths, perhaps without you ever becoming aware that this is happening. Less effective teachers treat all learners in the same way.

For all instruments there is a wide range of published tutor books or methods, and for the more popular instruments these may run into dozens of volumes. Choosing your own tutor book or method is very difficult, and in any case, most teachers have particular favourites which they use regularly. No matter how well written the book is, it may not adapt easily to your individual needs, and this is where a teacher's intervention is invaluable.

It's worth spending a moment thinking back to your own school days, and the lessons which you enjoyed and the ones you found less enjoyable. The probability is that the ones you enjoyed more, catered better for your learning needs. Think about your approach to assembling flat-pack furniture: are you naturally methodical? Do you lay out all the bits and pieces and check them off against the list, then read all the instructions before attempting to build the item? Or do you simply dive in and start work? Whatever your favoured approach to learning and doing, it's important that your teacher can work with you in this way.

One school of thought identifies three approaches to learning: visual, auditory and kinaesthetic, often referred to as VAK. Auditory learners prefer to hear instructions; visual learners prefer written or drawn communication; kinaesthetic learners prefer doing it and finding out. Interestingly, musical performance itself is often a combination of all three. The manipulation of the instrument means that certain movements are associated with certain sounds. In turn, these sounds become associated with visual images on the page – in other words, musical notation. Some learners prefer to process information first, before attempting something practical, whereas others simply want to start doing the activity straightaway.

There are no rights and wrongs here, simply a recognition that different individuals learn in different ways. If a teacher cannot or will not accept this, it is nothing more than a matter of luck as to whether their teaching style will match your needs as a learner. It's important not to be afraid of playing something wrongly: if you harbour this feeling you will find yourself for ever stopping, and so your music-making will lack continuity. It's better to keep going and make a mental note of what went wrong or where the problems occur, so that you can then go back and focus on the challenging bars.

Although an approach to teaching based on understanding VAK learning is popular with many, there is a counter argument which says that we all approach learning, and making sense of the world, through *all* our senses. Perhaps the key point here is that learners are most likely to benefit from teaching that adopts a range of strategies to help them overcome difficulties as they arise. The American educationalist Howard Gardner has advanced a theory of multiple intelligences, first published in *Frames of Mind* (1983), in which he puts forward the idea that we know the world through seven intelligences, one of which is musical thinking, and that it is the combination of strengths that we have in these different intelligences which makes us function differently when in learning mode.

Current research indicates that in order to learn something effectively you need to be able to switch from a very focused approach to one where learning takes place in the background. We are all familiar with encountering a particular problem where we feel unsure of the best course of action: the expression that comes to mind is 'I'll sleep on it and decide what to do in the morning.' Many people will have experienced the feeling of waking up the next morning and knowing what to do, feeling confident about moving forwards. That works because while we are asleep our brain tackles the problem without focusing on it. When coupled with the idea of repetition with spaces in between, it can be a highly effective way of tackling skill acquisition, and it works well for music.

Balancing that approach is the idea of being 'mindful', or very thoughtful about the way that something challenging is approached. This will involve breaking down the thing that we find difficult into smaller chunks and mastering each one before going on to the next. There's no doubt that a mixed approach, using all these strategies, is likely to be most beneficial to us as learners.

Where possible, we should all be encouraged to develop our learning across all learning styles. There may be a need to read and obey instructions, to write examination answers, and most certainly to respond to visual signals if we make music with other people. Good instrumental teaching will help you develop skills in all these areas.

MUSIC AND THE MIND

No matter how far back we travel in history, it is evident that music has been something more to mankind than mere sounds that are found to be pleasing to listen to, dance to, or march to. Let's take a brief look at some of the areas and a few of the individuals that we can identify.

People who lived in the upper palaeolithic time, 10,000–40,000 years ago, lived in caves, and researchers have found that within such caves the wall areas that were painted also matched the most resonant parts of the cave systems. We believe that the paintings were part of a ritual system, and bone flutes, whistles and stone chimes, known as lithophones, have also been found, often close to the most resonant parts of these chambers and close to the wall paintings. This research suggests that music played a part in ritual all those thousands of years ago.

The ancient Greeks took great interest in music, and it is written about frequently by Plato and was the subject of much research by Pythagoras, who used mathematics to analyse features of vibration and sound. Bach, in addition to being a prolific composer, was a numerologist, and there are references throughout his work to the relationship between mathematics and musical composition. It is argued by some historians that he sought to base some of his compositions on the golden section, the ratio that is referred to in ancient Greece and was set out by the mathematician Euclid. Its application is also found in Renaissance art.

Claude Levi Strauss (1908–2009), the French anthropologist and ethnologist, wrote at length about music and myth and said:

> Since music is a language with some meaning at least for the immense majority of mankind, although only a tiny minority of people are capable of formulating a meaning in it, and since it is the only language with the contradictory attributes of being at once intelligible and untranslatable, the musical creator is a being comparable to the gods, and music itself the supreme mystery of the science of man, a mystery that all the various disciplines come up against and which holds the key to their progress.

The neurologist Oliver Sachs (1933–2015) in his book *Musicophilia*, published in 2008, provides many curious examples of how music has entered the lives of adults, suddenly and completely unexpectedly. He also explored synaesthesia, the condition experienced by some people where they see sounds as colour, although it seems there is no common pattern to the way that individuals relate different colours to pitches.

In the 1960s, Hungary implemented an approach to music education developed by the Hungarian composer Zoltan Kodaly, and it is still in place in Hungary today. This has led to high standards of music in schools for the vast majority of children, and it has also put the country ahead in league tables of academic achievement.

The apparent phenomenon known as 'the Mozart effect' refers to the idea that for some time music teachers and some parents have believed that studying music makes children and young people cleverer. In his book *The Mozart Effect*, published in 2007, Don Campbell set out the view that listening to music by Mozart can 'heal the body, strengthen the mind and unlock the creative spirit'. Although subsequent research seems to cast some doubt on his findings, nevertheless a large number of people believe passionately in the value of playing Mozart to pregnant mothers and to very young children, and it does seem to be the case that classical music played in the background can aid concentration for some learners.

The reality is that we are all different, and what may be true for one learner isn't necessarily true for the next.

Healthcare professionals now use music to stimulate motor function in patients whose nerves have been impaired by stroke or Parkinson's disease, and some farmers play music to increase milk production in their dairy cows. There seems little or no doubt that musicking does something to humans and animals alike.

ACCESS

There are no grounds for anyone to feel that they are excluded from learning to play a musical instrument. There are some 1.5 million people in the UK with a learning disability, and inclusivity is now an important part of UK educational policy and enactment. Of course, careful thought should be given to practical matters if you have a physical disability, in the same way that fragility, or otherwise, of the instrument and relative difficulty, in terms of mastery of it, should also be considered.

If you have a visual impairment there is helpful advice readily available from organizations such as the Royal National Institute of Blind People, and similarly for those with hearing impairment from Action on Hearing Loss (the name for the Royal National Institute for the Deaf since 2011). You may wish to find a teacher who specializes in working with learners who have a disability.

In recent years there has been exciting research at the Massachusetts Institute of Technology (MIT) on enabling adults with disabilities such as cerebral palsy, to express themselves through music-making, composition and performance. It is often research work such as this that leads to focused outcomes, encouraging software developers and programmers to create apps that increase and broaden access for all individuals.

Most private teachers, even if their experience of working with learners with special needs is not extensive, will be open to exploring how things can be made to work. Instrumental teachers who also work in schools will be able to get advice and support from a school and/or local authority.

Learning to play an instrument may have a therapeutic benefit for any learner, but this should not be confused with music therapy itself, which has a different purpose. Music therapy is an established clinical discipline which involves a professional music therapist working with an individual to help improve their mental and/or physical health. It is not focused on enabling the recipient to acquire musical understanding and skills, although that may to some extent occur as part of the therapeutic process.

A BRIEF HISTORICAL OVERVIEW OF MUSIC EDUCATION

You may be very aware of the reasons why you didn't take up music as a child, but regardless of your personal and family circumstances, the place of music in education may also have played a part. This short section takes a look at that aspect of music in learners' lives, and though far from comprehensive, it may open up some new thinking for you and may even encourage you to find out more about music education in the past as a way of understanding the best way forwards now, for you.

With a focus on Western classical tradition we need go back no further than the fifteenth century, and the development of printed musical notation, to witness some of the key historical features. In the middle of the fifteenth century Gutenburg invented the printing press. Soon afterwards it was adapted to print music, and it is this development that led to the spread of interest in musical study and the growth of musical composition. By the middle to late sixteenth century there was a steadily increasing demand for sheet music, and with it came a matching demand for instrumental and vocal tuition.

In turn, this led to the publication of a number of instrumental tutors. Notable amongst these publications was Thomas Morley's *A Plain and Easie Introduction to Practical Music* (1597). Morley (1557–1602) may have been a friend of Shakespeare, and composed many madrigals. The publication of his tutor book came just a few years after William Byrd's observations on the value of singing, quoted earlier in this book (see Chapter 1). Castiglione in his treatise 'The Courtier', published in 1528, which describes a perfect renaissance gentleman, states that the young courtier should be able to read music and play several instruments. Music, he says, is not an ornament, but a necessity.

Moving to the seventeenth century, in 1654 John Playford published his *A Breefe Introduction to the Skill of Musick*, which encompassed musical theory, instructions and lessons for the bass viol and treble violin, and musical composition.

Amongst the great composers, Bach (1685–1750) himself was an experienced teacher. For much of his life he worked as a Kapellmeister, which involved composing for weekly and other church services, rehearsing and conducting the choir and playing the organ. Among his large output as a composer is music for beginners, such as the Anna Magdalena notebooks, written in 1722 and 1725 for his second wife.

As an adult, thinking about which musical instrument you would like to learn, what happened one hundred or more years ago may seem irrelevant. But the reality is that you may well find yourself learning pieces written in those days, such as the Bach Minuet in G from the Anna Magdalena notebook, and through methods and principles that were first set out during Victorian times. While some of this thinking is highly pertinent to today's learning environment, some has impacted in a negative way on today's teaching.

The approach of many musicians to instrumental and vocal teaching in the nineteenth, twentieth and twenty-first centuries traces its origins back to the master apprentice. Essentially, this advocated putting a group of learners in a 'masterclass' situation in the presence of a good or great player. The weakness in this methodology is that the good or great player may not be a good, or even reasonably good, teacher. The system relies on self-motivated learners who are also good problem solvers, and can thrive in this often competitive environment. Whilst it does produce some good players, it also keeps their number small.

Second, let's look at the rise of music, choral singing, piano and violin lessons in Victorian society, and give some thought to the numerous inventions of late Victorian England. During the nineteenth century there was a big increase in the number of professional musicians in Britain. Amongst those who taught music there was a clear shift from male dominance to female dominance during this period, and you can read much more about this in Cyril Ehrlich's fascinating book, *The Music Profession in Britain since the Eighteenth Century.*

Victorian Britain also saw the development and growth of leisuretime pursuits, which included participation in music or listening to music as a concert goer, or attending one of the many music halls that were opening up. Music was seen as a force for good amongst social reformers. Ehrlich quotes an advertisement for the Preston Vocal and Instrumental Society of 1835, offering 'a rational and pleasing course of evening recreation, apart from the seductive influence of the tavern'.

In 1837 the eighteen-year-old Victoria was crowned Queen, and the start of her reign coincided with the development of colour lithography. This cheaper form of printing meant the opportunity to produce more method books, a shift partly away from the aural tradition of teaching and a move to placing greater emphasis on the development of technical skills linked to the study of notation. The player-teachers working at the higher levels saw the opportunity to market their own methods through the publication of tutor books. They could compose their own pieces and studies in addition to including technical exercises and musical rudiments. Importantly, these method books associated fingers with notation, rather than fingers with sounds.

In 1841, John Hullah's book for schoolmasters on singing was published, and the following year, no fewer than fifty thousand teachers attended his classes to learn how to teach singing. Hullah, government inspector for music, was convinced that 'music contained within it a moral force which could refine and cultivate individuals and encourage a sense of value and worth within the community'. In 1874 he published *Time and Tune in the Elementary School.*

The importance of music and music teaching is exemplified in the area of school music with this quote from Ehrlich's book: 'In 1878 government spending was estimated at £100,000 from the practice of granting schools one shilling per head if inspectors reported that singing was "part of the ordinary course of instruction".' A later modification allowed sixpence for singing 'by ear' and one shilling 'at sight'.

In the mid-nineteenth century there was a rise in choral singing. The Rev. John Curwen (1816–80), building on – or, as some may view it, taking from – the work of Sarah Glover, adapted an existing form of sol-fa, and developed the tonic sol-fa modulator, which used hand signs related to pitch: these are similar to the ones used by the Hungarian, Kodaly, a century later. Curwen had found music reading difficult, but saw the value of it in terms of encouraging the children who attended his Sunday School to sing hymns. He established a tonic sol-fa college and a publishing company, J. Curwen and Sons, to assist in the propagation of his belief in the sol-fa method. The method was officially adopted by the English Education Department in 1860, and the sol-fa movement gathered a huge following. From your own school days, you may even remember seeing a big chart hanging on the classroom wall – the tonic sol-fa modulator – as these charts were commonplace in schools until the third quarter of the last century.

The piano increased in popularity throughout the Victorian era with modestly priced instruments being widely available from around 1880 onwards. Many were sold on a hire purchase scheme, and the manufacturing quality was sufficient to ensure the development of a strong secondhand market. By 1900 there were one hundred piano makers in London alone, and perhaps as many as one instrument per ten amongst the population.

Annie Gregg (1845–1932) was born in Dublin, and after graduating from the Royal Irish Academy of Music she moved to Scotland where she met the music educator, the Rev. John Curwen (1816–80, see above). Annie married John Curwen's eldest son, and in 1886 she published *Mrs. Curwen's Pianoforte Method (The Child Pianist) Being a Practical Course of the Elements of Music*, which ran to at least twenty editions, along with the publication of a separate volume, *The Teacher's Guide*, a companion to her method books (see Recommended Reading). In the teacher's book, Mrs Curwen set out the following maxims:

1. Teach the easy before the difficult.
2. Teach the thing before the sign.
3. Teach one fact at a time, and the commonest fact first.
4. Leave out all exceptions and anomalies until the general rule is understood.
5. In training the mind, teach the concrete before the abstract.
6. In developing physical skill, teach the elemental before the compound, and do one thing at a time.
7. Proceed from the known to the related unknown.
8. Let each lesson, as far as possible, rise out of that which goes before and lead up to that which follows.

9. Call in the understanding to help the skill at every step.
10. Let the first impression be a correct one; leave no room for misunderstanding.
11. Never tell a pupil anything that you can help him to discover for himself.
12. Let the pupil as soon as possible derive some pleasure from his knowledge. Interest can only be kept up by a sense of growth in independent power.

These principles could just as well be applied to teaching and learning today, and you may find it instructive to compare any music teaching you have encountered, at any point in your life, with these thoughts, and of course, to compare the work of a teacher with whom you are learning now, or going to start learning.

Since the introduction of the electronic keyboard in the early 1980s, there has been a steady decline in both the piano manufacturing industry in the UK and in the number of children and young people learning the instrument. This is in marked contrast to China, where in 2012, some 380,000 pianos were manufactured, representing one piano every three urban households. China has maybe forty million children and young people learning to play the piano, and has witnessed a rapid growth of interest in graded music exams.

Towards the end of the nineteenth century a new fashion developed, which meant a significant increase in numbers learning to play the violin. In 1889 the Japanese manufacturer Suzuki opened their first factory in Tokyo, and it is thought that this may have been after a visit to the UK, where they may have seen the 'Maidstone' movement in action. The growth of interest in violin playing in the UK was led in some respects by the activity of one UK commercial business: Murdoch's. Thomas Mee Pattison (1845–1936), musical adviser of the London-based J. G. Murdoch & Co., music publishing house and instrument manufacturer, enlisted the support of his company to promote violin class instruction for schoolchildren by providing all the supplies needed: violins, teaching materials and teachers, for one inclusive, inexpensive price. Students were allowed to pay for their violin outfits in instalments, generally at a cost of one shilling per week.

This whole class teaching method was named in honour of the first group violin class to experiment with this approach: the All Saints' National School in Maidstone, England, sometimes known as the Maidstone Movement. In 1897, the Murdoch Company formed the Maidstone School Orchestra Association (MSOA) to promote their method. At the height of the MSOA's popularity, 400,000 British schoolchildren – one in ten of the state school population – participated in Maidstone School Orchestra classes.

Finally, in our brief historical overview, let's take a look at some developments in music education in the twentieth century. In the early years of the twentieth century the National Union of School Orchestras was formed in 1905, and at its 1914 annual music festival, held at the Crystal Palace, 3,650 intermediate students were featured performing en masse. These statistics provide an indication of the popularity of learning music over one hundred years ago. After World War II we see the rise of the local education authority (LEA), from the 1950s. Each LEA appointed a music adviser, and most LEAs established Music Services to provide free tuition to selected learners. The allocation of peripatetic instrumental teachers to schools was essentially modelled on the needs of the symphony orchestra, with proportionate allocations of teaching time for strings, woodwind, brasswind and percussion. Woodwind, brasswind and percussion often started in the secondary school, and children and young people who were learning were encouraged to join their school orchestra with a view to auditioning for the county youth orchestra or windband if they were good enough. Those at the very top of the tree would audition for the National Youth Orchestra (founded in 1948) which remains a very active educational institution today.

It was often the case that selection for the opportunity to learn an instrument free of charge, at school, was based on perceived musical aptitude. In one sense this seems rational given that unlimited resources, instruments and teachers, were not available. The reality was that many children missed out on the chance to learn to play because they were unable to demonstrate some aural musical perception at that initial testing stage. Perhaps something like this happened to you at school?

In the 1960s, music educators sought to find a way to overcome this unfairness in the selection process. Dr Arnold Bentley (1913–2001), at Reading University, devised a series of tests specifically for the purpose, and he also advocated the adoption of John Curwen's sol-fa method as a means of teaching sight singing in schools. There has recently been a resurgence of interest in Bentley's musical aptitude tests, and while they may provide an indication of a learner's musical perception at a given stage, they do not, of course, provide any indication of whether a learner will persevere with the learning of their instrument, which, it may be argued, is actually more important, particularly for children and young people at school.

In 1988 the first GCSE students sat the new examination, and in the same year, the Education Reform Act ushered in the country's first national curriculum. Part of the Act's intention was the delegation of centrally held funding to be diverted from LEAs directly to schools. One of the unintended consequences of this was the gradual decline in Music Services, first in terms of their ability to employ instrumental teachers, and later in terms of their very existence. This began with the introduction of modest charges to parents of children in receipt of instrumental lessons, but by the mid-1990s there was a huge variance in the amounts being charged across the country for music lessons.

It was not until the Labour government introduced the Standards Fund in 1999, with the intention of saving Music Services, that the tide began to turn back in favour of Music Services' work, and the first decade of this century saw an unprecedented amount of activity in music education, much of it government backed or led. In 2000, the Secretary of State for Education, David Blunkett, pledged that over time all children of primary school age should have the opportunity to learn a musical instrument. A survey the following year showed that no more than 8 per cent of school age children were having regular tuition on a musical instrument – that is, about 500,000 pupils. Significantly, this figure is no greater than the numbers learning through the Maidstone movement a hundred years earlier.

In the same year, as part of a series of measures to counteract this decline in instrumental learning, six local education authorities were invited by the Department for Education and Skills (DfES) to participate in a pilot programme to show how specialist instrumental tuition could be used in a whole class or large group environment to enable larger numbers of children to experience music learning at first hand. This experiment led to an announcement of increased government funding to enable all Music Services in England to roll out programmes of whole class instrumental/vocal tuition in 2007. Meanwhile in 2004, the government launched its 'Music Manifesto', which aimed to bring together a broad range of individuals and organizations interested in music education. It was described by the then Schools Minister, David Miliband, as 'a route map for the future of music in schools'.

Although there was a dramatic increase in the number of children seen to be having instrumental lessons, the potential for growth was short-lived, as in 2006 the funding of £26 million was given directly to schools to spend as they wished, rather than being channelled directly into music provision. The other flaw in the scheme to increase participation was that up to a year of instrumental tuition, plus the instrument, was provided free, but for those children who wished to continue with lessons after that initial period, parents were expected to make a financial contribution. Some children were reluctant to move from the fun of whole class learning to having lessons in a small group, and some parents were unable or unwilling to make the necessary financial commitment. The government target was that by 2011, 1.15 million children should have experienced a period of tuition on an instrument, as against the 438,772 learning in 2005.

Against this flurry of initiatives and intense activity amongst Music Services, there was growing evidence of a substantial number of more advanced young players coming from independent schools, rather than maintained ones. Thus instrumental tuition had remained the province of those who were deemed to have musical aptitude, and those whose parents could afford to buy tuition. The National Youth Orchestra of Great Britain (NYO) provides a snapshot of the shortcomings in music education. The NYO is made up of thirteen-to nineteen-year-olds, and is the premier music ensemble for young people. It enjoys an international reputation, undertaking overseas tours and giving high profile concerts, including an annual appearance at the BBC Proms, but in December 2010, the Times Educational Supplement reported that less than half of the 526 applicants for places in the NYO came from maintained schools.

In 2011, against this backdrop, Darren Henley, the then CEO of Classic FM Radio, was invited to undertake a review of music education in England, and in 2011 his National Plan for Music Education (NPME) was launched. In the following year, 2012, music hubs were launched in England with a view to bringing together organizations engaging in music-making for children and young people. The Arts Council has been given responsibility for managing hubs, and describes them in these terms:

> Music education hubs include schools – from primary to further education institutions – professional music organisations and arts organisations. They work in local areas to bring people together to create joined-up music education provision for children and young people.
>
> We expect every child to have the opportunity to sing, play instruments, solo and in groups, and to be able to take these skills further if they have the talent or inspiration.
>
> The hubs are a new way of organising music education, and have now been in place for two school years. Already, these hubs

are working with 80 per cent of schools in England, meaning that around one million children and young people are learning a musical instrument.

In a lecture given at the Guildhall School of Music and Drama in 2001, distinguished music educator, Professor John Paynter (1931–2010), who championed the cause of creativity and practical music-making in the classroom, said this about music in the school curriculum:

> In spite of centuries of experience and experiment, the practicalities and benefits of a general education – schooling – remain uncertain. Can we sustain the spread of subjects that now make up the curriculum? In particular, can we justify time spent on music, which to many would appear to be a specialised study for the talented? The evidence of past practice suggests that the content of classroom music teaching has not done much to help the majority of people to understand music. Yet making music is manifestly an important feature of our humanity. Are there principles at work deep in the nature of music which explain this, and can these features be exploited as the basis of a musical education which will have value for everyone?

Although this is no more than a thumbnail sketch of some features of music education, it may help to draw attention to factors which perhaps influenced your learning and experiences of music as a child or young person, and perhaps enable you to account for the fact that you didn't take up an instrument earlier in your life. Perhaps learning to play a musical instrument wasn't commonplace in your school or home environment. Perhaps to do so was financially out of reach, or maybe you were actively put off the idea of participation in music through the learning experiences you had at school. But whatever your background and past experience, now is the time to alter course and continue your journey in a new direction, with music to help you on your way.

CHAPTER 6

Practical Matters

Most new hobbies or interests involve a financial outlay of some sort. It is as well to give that, and other practical matters, some thought before you start, to ease your passage on the journey that you are keen to begin. It is also important to try and narrow down the style or genre of music you want to play.

Try answering these questions to help you think about your preferences:

- What sort of music do you particularly like to listen to?
- Is this the sort of music you would like to play?
- Have you tried listening to a broad range of music to be sure about what you like?
- Have you talked about your idea of learning an instrument with your partner or a friend?
- Do you have a budget in mind for your exploration of practical music-making?

THE QUESTION OF FINANCE

Embarking on learning a musical instrument may represent a significant financial commitment, although there can be little doubt that the benefits should far outweigh the expense. However, it may help if you give some thought to the following costs, any of which you are likely to incur:

- payment for lessons
- hiring or buying an instrument
- buying a music stand
- buying sheet music
- replacing reeds/strings and so on
- accessories, for example mutes, music stand, tuner, metronome
- maintenance/tuning of the instrument
- joining an ensemble
- attending a music centre

- subscribing to a music journal
- subscription for a music association

And looking further ahead:

- entering exams, competitions, festivals
- concert wear
- study or holiday courses
- concert tours
- transport to and from lessons and rehearsals
- time

On the plus side you will benefit from your encounter with music-making, no matter how brief: you will develop a range of transferable skills, including improvement in co-operation, concentration, listening and co-ordination, and also fine motor skills; and you will almost certainly develop new friendship groups. There is substantial evidence from research to show that participating in music is beneficial to health and well-being in a variety of ways.

Instrumental lessons are usually provided at your music teacher's home, although some teachers may be willing to travel to your address if you have a suitable space for the lesson to take place. Of course, if you are learning the piano, you probably don't have too much choice about where your instrument will be located within your house. If, on the other hand, you are learning a woodwind, brasswind or stringed instrument, you may be able to play it in a number of different rooms, and, taking care not to annoy your neighbours, it can be well worthwhile exploring the acoustic response from different rooms. A heavily carpeted living room with sofas, other soft furnishings and curtains drawn will provide an acoustically unresponsive place to play in, whereas a kitchen, which is likely to have a hard floor surface and few soft furnishings, will be an acoustically flattering environment. If your instrument is portable and you feel that the sound you are producing is rather dull and lacklustre, just try playing in some different acoustics to check if it is your tone production, or the environment, which bears most of the responsibility.

BUYING OR RENTING AN INSTRUMENT

Before purchasing a new or secondhand instrument it is essential to try it out. There can be a world of difference between one model of an instrument and another, in terms of cost, and also in terms of sound and ease of sound production. Some instruments 'speak' more easily for no truly apparent reason. In any event, never buy, or rent, an instrument without first consulting your teacher. Some teachers may have preferences for one make of instrument over another, while some may not be willing to teach on a particular make of instrument. Borrowing someone's clarinet that they had lessons on 'way back when' is equally risky, as your teacher may be reluctant to tell you that it is now almost unplayable.

Buying a secondhand instrument, as with buying anything secondhand, is a more risky business and you would do well to take an expert with you, preferably your instrumental teacher if they are willing to help. What might seem like a bargain could need costly repairs in the near future; it could be tuned to a different pitch, or be inappropriate for a beginner, or be harder to play than an instrument designed for a beginner. Equally risky to making a secondhand purchase is when a kindly relative promises to supply an instrument as a gift. Again, it is always best to have any instrument vetted or chosen by your teacher, or teacher-to-be. You can always 'blame' your teacher if you need to reject a kind gift or turn away an unmissable bargain.

Many instrument dealers operate rental schemes that offer some form of discount if you buy the instrument at a later date. This can be an ideal way of setting up an opportunity to learn on a better quality instrument for a term or two, before committing to actually buying one. Buying an instrument at an auction, either live or online, is equally risky unless you really know what you are doing, and have either your teacher's backing or real-time support for what you are doing. As a beginner you may not be able to thoroughly test an instrument that you would like to buy, and without a proper 'road' test it is difficult to be sure that you are doing the right thing.

As with purchasing anything new, most dealers will offer attractive discounts to first-time buyers with nothing to trade in. The advantage of the rental instrument is that it can be traded in/ updated as needs be. Once the purchase or rental of your instrument is complete, make sure that it is included on an appropriate household or musical instrument insurance policy. Remember that your normal household insurance may not cover your instrument when you take it by car, bus, train or on foot, to and from your lessons or rehearsals. Check your car insurance too, and find out whether your own insurance will cover the instrument in transit and away from home. A number of firms specialize in musical instrument insurance.

BUYING PRINTED MUSIC

Some teachers will buy the printed music – often known as sheet music – that you will need, and then collect payment from you. Others are unwilling or unable to do this. Whilst there is nothing to beat browsing the shelves of your local music shop, you may prefer to purchase online, and this is an efficient way of dealing with the matter. Most experienced teachers are cost conscious, so will not expect their students to keep purchasing new pieces of music, or to buy one expensive album and then only study one piece from it.

Photocopying music is illegal in almost all circumstances, so it is unwise to accept photocopies from a teacher – in any event, they should not be giving such copies to learners. By purchasing sheet music and supporting publishers you are enabling the publishing industry to survive financially, and thus commission new works from composers, and keep costs down. If you feel that the music you are being asked to pay for is too expensive, ask the teacher if there is a choice of publisher or edition.

As regards exam music there will nearly always be a choice, and in the case of straightforward teaching material it should be possible to choose a more cost-effective item. The exceptions to this are those instruments that have a smaller repertoire of music published for them – the harp is a good example, where many pieces are very expensive. At the other end of the scale there is a wide range of music for clarinet and flute, which is very modestly priced. You will benefit from developing your own collection of music: it can last a lifetime, and may even be appropriate for your own children or grandchildren to play in years to come.

MUSIC RETAILERS

It is getting harder to find music dealerships in the UK, especially ones that stock sheet music and have more of a focus on classical music, as the online market takes over. Almost the reverse is true in south-east Asia where the music retail business flourishes and many shops not only sell instruments and sheet music, but are also centres for tuition and performance.

Good retailers will stock a broad range of music, including exam pieces and the syllabuses of various exam boards. They get to know teachers in the neighbourhood, and they know what sells best, and which pieces, and albums of music, the more effective teachers are purchasing. They are therefore well placed to offer advice – but music should rarely be purchased without seeking your teacher's advice first. There is nothing worse for a teacher than to be confronted by a beginner clutching a piece of music that they desperately want to play, but which the teacher knows is way beyond their ability at that stage. Of course, the sheet music will keep until the time your technique has caught up with your aspirations, and a good teacher may direct you to a simplified version of the piece you have chosen. Indeed, an internet search may reveal a number of options that will enable you to access the music you would really like to play.

Retailers are also a good source of Christmas and birthday gifts, and stock many accessories such as metronomes, electronic tuners, stationery and music cases. Online retail now provides a simple and efficient way of purchasing music and accessories such as reeds and strings; however, it is only suitable for buying an instrument if the journey to the shop is well nigh impossible, and only if you have already consulted your teacher about your proposed purchase.

MUSIC TECHNOLOGY: SOFTWARE AND APPS

It is easy to see why some music teachers have chosen to ignore music technology, which for others is an essential part of their daily existence. For some instruments, music technology is an integral part of the playing itself – for example, electronic keyboards or electronic drum kit or electric guitar. For an instrument such as the violin, music technology can play a supporting rôle for both learner and teacher. Some great classical violinists – for example Nigel Kennedy, who has also explored numerous other music genres – relish the additional effects they can access by playing an electric violin.

One of the driving forces in the development of musical technology in the last quarter of the twentieth century was MIDI – Musical Instrument Digital Interface, which was standardized in 1983. Miraculously, when electronic keyboards were being developed in the early 1980s, manufacturers agreed to use a standard means of connecting equipment from different sources together, called MIDI. By being able to transfer sound digitally, it is possible to take sound and turn it into notation: hence the development of notation software, which can respond to signals from a MIDI keyboard. Although MIDI has slightly taken a back seat, having been superseded by many other digital advances, it has paved the way for digital file transfer – and it is now of course possible for the teacher or student to send a music sound file by email; perhaps your teacher can send you a backing track to practise with, for example.

Recent developments in music technology include recorded accompaniments that keep in time with the solo instrument. So, for example, a trumpet player can practise a piece written for trumpet and piano by simply using a computer to play the recorded piano part, which will speed up or slow down in response to your trumpet playing. This would allow you, as the solo instrumentalist, to learn the piece as a whole, rather than just learning your part in isolation. It has the added advantage of providing an accompaniment for the learning of scales, and a 'looping' facility, controlled by the player, which allows you to repeat a few bars of music over and over again during practice. Musical notation software is readily available, even as a free download, allowing teachers and learners to notate their own music, either entering each note on the stave, or by playing a midi keyboard, or other midi-linked instrument, from which the computer program can transcribe the sound.

In recent years, software has been put into second place by apps, which are really nothing more than focused items of programming marketed separately for the end user. There is an app for almost everything musical you could wish to do. It is now possible to download a four-track recording app for free, whereas not so long ago you would have needed an expensive piece of hardware to do the same job. There are many metronome and tuner apps, and sampled sounds are also readily accessible.

HYGIENE

Issues of hygiene apply particularly to all woodwind and brasswind instruments, and are, in fact, important across the board. Instruments that involve putting the mouthpiece or reed on the lips or inside the mouth should not be shared with other players. If it is necessary for an instrument to be passed from one player to another, the mouthpiece should be disinfected. For brass instruments and recorders and flutes this is straightforward, but where reeds are involved it becomes more difficult, as any disinfectant may itself change the playing quality of the reed. You should expect your teacher to lead by example, and learners should be discouraged from allowing other friends and family members to 'have a blow' on their woodwind or brasswind instruments.

There are learning situations where woodwind or brasswind instruments are shared, for example, in whole class learning environments in schools. This can be done safely and hygienically by ensuring that each player has their own reed and mouthpiece for clarinets and saxophones, their own reed for oboes and bassoons, and their own mouthpiece for their brass instrument. Teachers will advise on how to keep the inside of the instrument clean. All such matters of hygiene become particularly important when coughs and colds are prevalent.

Although less a matter of hygiene and more a matter of plain cleanliness, it is a very good habit to wash your hands thoroughly before playing any instrument – and of course it is pianos and keyboards that show the evidence of failing to do this more quickly than most.

CHAPTER 7

The World of Music and Music-Making

Most people make music because they love being involved in it, rather than as their primary source of income. In other words, they are involved at an amateur or semi-professional level. The number of full-time professional musicians in the UK is small, and in a report published in 2012, the Musicians' Union stated that over half of the musicians they surveyed earned less than £20,000 per annum, and that 60 per cent reported that they had worked for free in the previous twelve months. On the other hand, the number of music teachers is much larger, though their income levels are still not high, even if they may be able to command more consistency in terms of income generation, particularly if they are good at what they do.

The work of teachers who give instrumental and vocal lessons in the UK is not regulated. The only teachers in this group whose work is regulated in any way are those who work for Music Services, or who are on a school's payroll. One of the consequences of this is that it is difficult to give precise numbers of individuals engaged in this form of work at any given time. There are over 24,000 schools in the UK, and something like 12,000 teachers working in music hubs, which does not account for the large number of teachers working privately. A conservative estimate suggests there could be 50,000 or more music teachers in the UK.

All of this has some relevance to you as an adult would-be learner of music because it is the world that you are about to enter. Even though you may have no aspirations to play music at a semi-professional, let alone professional level, you will be encountering part of this world through your teacher and the people that you meet, who are making music on a regular basis. Within the world of music there are numerous layers and groupings of activity, and we will explore just some of these.

PROFESSIONAL AND SEMI-PROFESSIONAL CLASSICAL MUSIC-MAKING

The number of musicians involved in professional music-making in what may be categorized as classical music – in other words symphony orchestras, opera houses and ballet companies – is relatively modest. Within the UK there are five BBC orchestras, seven orchestras that employ their players on full-time salaries, and seven orchestras that have fixed membership but employ players on a contract basis. In addition, there are thirteen opera or ballet companies that employ full-time musicians on a contract basis. There are a large number, around twenty-five, chamber orchestras, about ten orchestras that use period instruments, and some five or six contemporary ensembles.

Given a UK population of some sixty-four million in 2013, it doesn't need much mathematical acumen to realize that opportunities for professional musicians are few, and it is much more likely for a musician to find work as a freelance player than be engaged in a full-time salaried post. The situation on mainland Europe is rather different, with many countries having more full-time orchestras and opera houses with resident orchestras.

The semi-professional world of classical music-making is comprised of freelance players, many of whom are teachers working in independent schools, or for Music Services, or as private teachers. They often rehearse and perform music in the same way that the full-time professional musician does, that is to say, with a minimum amount of rehearsal time, a huge dependency on the excellence of their sight-reading skills, and usually very high standards of performance. A local choral society may present two or three performances per year with regular weekly rehearsals for the chorus, and they will be accompanied in performance by an orchestra of local semi-professionals who may have just one or possibly two, three-hour rehearsals immediately prior to a performance.

PROFESSIONAL OTHER THAN CLASSICAL MUSIC-MAKING

The classical music world may be a relatively small one, but alongside it the world of popular music is enormous and a massive generator of income for the UK economy. Until the 1960s, professional recording studios often had a small number of classically trained musicians as a house orchestra to provide backings for singers. With the emergence of the electric guitar and the move to the typical pop group format of lead singer, lead guitar, rhythm guitar, electric bass guitar and drums, the need for any kind of orchestral or ensemble backing has rapidly diminished.

In addition to the pop megastars there are hundreds of semi-professional musicians making music in function or gig bands, playing at dinner dances on two or more evenings per week. Here the emphasis is on giving performances of music, originally recorded by well known pop groups, which are familiar to the audience. Musical material from the 1960s onwards is likely to feature in this form of entertainment.

Alongside these semi-professional performers is another group of musicians, who get together to play jazz. The number of professional performers in this genre is comparatively small, as is the number of semi-professionals. For the latter group this tends to be the least likely to attract a meaningful pay level.

Musicians working in the classical, pop or jazz environments, be it as professionals, semi-professionals or unpaid amateurs, have almost all experienced a long process of training to reach the standards they have attained. Although a small number of musicians working in popular music may be largely self-taught, the majority across all styles will probably have studied their instrument since childhood, perhaps taken many of the practical grades of music exam, and many will have studied music at a conservatoire or university. To maintain their high standards they engage regularly in music-making, and professionals will spend some time practising most days if they are not actually earning a living by playing music.

DECLINE IN THE TWENTIETH CENTURY

The twentieth century was a period of slow but steady decline in demand for professional musicians working across most genres. In the late 1920s, silent films which, in the best cinemas, had relied on a pit orchestra to provide music for the drama as it unfolded before people's eyes, were eclipsed almost instantly when *The Jazz Singer*, starring Al Jolson, with its synchronized dialogue, appeared in 1927. Although it was not the first movie to use synchronized sound, it heralded the end for silent movies, and within a very short space of time, pit orchestras for films were disbanded.

Following World War II, advances in recording soon led to the abandonment of the old shellac 78rpm disc, and its replacement, the vinyl 33rpm disc. Better recording of sound meant a slow decline in the demand for live music. For example, the holiday camps that developed from the nineteen-fifties onwards in the UK, all had resident bands for the summer season, and for many freelance musicians this was a time of guaranteed income for as long as six months. At the same time, television was gradually becoming affordable for more and more families. In its early post-war days, television shows involving music usually featured a live band or orchestra, but as this form of entertainment grew in popularity, the need for live musicians at local shows diminished.

The nineteen-eighties marked the dawn of the digital age. In 1983 a synthesizer was launched that was not only portable, but also featured a wide range of pre-programmed sounds that met the needs of many musicians. It also featured the new MIDI protocol, which made it easier to link it with other pieces of audio equipment. Musicians soon found that they could use a synthesizer to create a backing track, and provide high quality live music in performance with fewer musicians needed to play it. With the increase in digitization from the mid-1990s, and the spread of internet-based musical activity, there has been a further shift in the function of music played live. Digital downloads enable musical performances to be traded online, and most people listening to music will find it difficult to know whether the sounds they are hearing were created by live musicians or through digital manipulation. Today's smartphone, equipped with a few modestly priced apps, will enable you to do more in the way of music technology than would have been possible twenty-five years ago even with a substantial budget at your disposal.

The music industry is now recognized as a major contributor to the UK economy, with a value placed on it of between three and four billion pounds. On its website, UK Music states that this is made up of the following: '£1.6bn from musicians, composers and songwriters; £634m from recorded music; £662m from live music; £402m from music publishing; £151m from music representatives; £80m from music producers, recording studios; £1.4bn the value of exports; 101,680 full-time jobs.' However, those values are very much connected with the commercial world of popular music-making, and are a long way from the very modestly priced lessons that enable the majority of music teachers to exist. Although there are hugely expensive areas of activity within the Western classical tradition of music, such as opera, the bulk of activity within the music education sector operates on a much lower scale of economic values.

MUSIC FOR THE AMATEUR

Although the picture of professional music-making may feel like a rather sad decline, the world of amateur music-making continues to flourish in the UK, and even has its own national charitable organization, Making Music, or the National Federation of Music Societies (NFMS) as it was known when it was founded in 1935. NFMS was created to support amateur music groups and to promote music education in the wake of the Depression, but music-making by unpaid non-professional musicians has long been a part of the UK's live music culture, and its history goes back a long way.

We have already seen that music was an accomplishment of Renaissance Man. Making music vocally has traditionally accompanied repetitive work, and instrumental and choral music-making flourished significantly in Victorian times with the development of working men's brass bands and the formation of large choral societies. The availability of relatively cheap printed sheet music developed alongside the growth of the choral tradition, and similarly led to the development of amateur orchestras across the whole of the UK.

Music has always been important to the military, and bandsmen on retirement from military service, might provide tuition for youngsters in their neighbourhood. Wherever there is a stable number of musicians, the secondhand instrument market will grow, which enables new learners to start and, in turn, leads to the formation of amateur ensembles, bands and orchestras.

The choral societies of Victorian times needed bands consisting of amateur and semi-professional players to accompany their performances, and that tradition continues today. As discussed above, the twentieth century has seen a steady decline in the number of opportunities for professional and semi-professional musicians: silent movies with their orchestral pit players replaced by 'talking films', pantomimes moving from a small orchestra to one or two musicians using a synthesizer and backing tracks, and summer season bands being replaced by duos or trios, and so on.

The knock-on effect of all this is an increase in the number of players who are not being paid a professional wage but are still keen to make music – and so amateur music-making flourishes. A quick internet search will reveal dozens of orchestras, bands and ensembles that meet regularly, and most welcome new players. The number of children learning musical instruments has increased since the middle of the last century, and significantly so recently, and this has created a large number of players of modest ability who are keen to continue making music after their schooldays are over.

MUSIC AS A PROFESSION

Of the many thousands of children and young people who begin to learn an instrument, very few will subsequently move into the music profession as performers. In the world of 'classical' music there are two key reasons for this: firstly, the number of vacancies for professional musicians is tiny; and secondly, performance standards are very high, and out of reach for all but a few learners, besides which the professional musician must have the temperament to deal with long hours, lots of travel, and the immense pressure of public performance.

For every player auditioned and selected to play in an orchestra there may be another fifty who are equally good, yet who are rejected. That said, some instruments attract fewer learners than others, and whereas there may be only two or three clarinetists employed in an orchestra, there will be many more violinists, violists, cellists and double bassists. In the world of popular music, success is as much to do with effective promotion and marketing as it is with pure musical ability. In short, there are no rules to guarantee success here.

Most children and young people will realize where they are in the pecking order of achievement. Exam or festival success, or otherwise, can help by providing an objective appraisal of performance, but sometimes it is necessary for a parent or teacher to explain to a learner that their long-term goal may be unattainable, and this should be done kindly, and in good time.

Children and young people who are making very good progress with their instrumental learning will probably join the local youth orchestra, and may wish to consider the National Youth Orchestra as an ultimate goal. In the UK, most of the music conservatoires run Saturday junior departments, which provide access to high quality musical experiences.

Another possibility for individuals who really want to play is the route of making music in a military band. The training provided will be as good as that in any other institution, and entrants are often required to gain expertise on a second instrument that is unrelated to their first. This broadens their musical outlook and helps them to understand a wider variety of music.

Of those children and young people who learn instruments associated with Western classical music, many do not continue with their music-making after leaving school. In one sense this mirrors the complete school process, which narrows down the number of subjects leading towards qualifications when the child is sixteen and then at eighteen, and then through higher education, towards eventual employment. For those who do continue, and for those who resume playing a little later, there is a rich seam of amateur and semi-professional music-making open to them. Thus musical encounters and experiences acquired through learning an instrument whilst at school should never be considered as time lost or wasted.

TRAVELLING AND TOURING AS A MUSICIAN

Musicians through history have faced the issue of travelling to their audience, from the composer/performer troubadours of the twelfth century, to the minstrels of the thirteenth to sixteenth centuries, and on to the mega tours of the twenty-first-century rock star and classical musician. Live performances of music demand new audiences, and in the years before sound recording was possible this meant that the musician always had to find new listeners to play to.

Today, children and young people who are regular members of bands and orchestras will often bring home a letter inviting them to take part, as a band member, on a tour to another country. In fact there are a number of tour operators who specialize in such work, not only organizing the travel and accommodation, but also arranging concerts at appropriate venues, and in some instances helping to guarantee audiences. Such trips are not confined to this age group, and many adult or mixed-age bands, orchestras and ensembles enjoy the exhausting and exhilarating fun to be had by combining music with travel.

For professional musicians, travelling is very much part of their working life, and most musicians enjoy it and look forward to visiting new places and making new friends. It may become a chore for those who find themselves making the same trip round a circuit of towns in the depths of winter, but a visit to another continent easily provides stimulating compensation.

It is worth noting that travelling and playing heightens the need to look after one's health, and there is a growing awareness of this amongst performers and teachers.

CHAPTER 8

Practical Tips

Trying to remember everything your teacher said during a lesson can be difficult, especially at the beginning of learning something new, when it can feel as if you are being bombarded with information. This chapter provides some simple common-sense reminders of some of the more important things.

GETTING STARTED ON YOUR INSTRUMENT

Let's start by taking a look at the piano, because this is the one instrument that makes a sound most easily. With the piano, it is vital that you adopt a comfortable sitting position, with your forearms parallel to the floor and your fingers slightly curled and ready to play, just above the white keys. Your teacher will, of course, help you during your lessons, but you need to be able to replicate this position at home. It may even be worth getting your teacher to take a photo of you in profile sitting at the piano, and then asking someone to help you to get this position right at home.

Sit towards the front edge of the piano stool, and if you don't have an adjustable stool, an easy way to make the sitting position a little higher is to use cushions or even samples of material that are comfortable to sit on; you can add them one at a time until you are sitting high enough. If you are playing on a grand piano, you may also need to experiment with the distance that the music stand is away from you, and at what angle you find it most comfortably positioned to enable you to see and read the notation easily. There are many helpful texts and video clips that you can refer to.

To help you feel confident about keyboard geography, try placing your hands in the correct position for the beginning of a piece, then close your eyes, put your hands on your lap, then put them back on the keyboard. You should soon find that if you have the stool in the right position your hands will be able to find the keys easily. All this is about feeling comfortable and being in a familiar position when you sit down and are getting ready to play.

If you are playing a woodwind instrument such as the flute, clarinet, oboe or saxophone, it is probably best to begin by standing up when you practise. The same can be said for trumpet, cornet and trombone, and for violin and viola from the string family. Although it may be a little more tiring to stand up, it is much easier to develop a proper and comfortable playing position when standing rather than sitting, unless you have a particular reason for sitting. At this stage you are unlikely to be playing for longer than twenty to thirty minutes at any one time, so standing should not be too much of a problem for most people. If you do need to sit down to practise, ask your teacher to help you find the best sitting position.

Some instruments, such as the cello, the larger brass instruments and the bassoon, are more commonly played in a sitting position, although almost all these instruments are also found in military marching bands and can be played whilst standing. Make sure you have a comfortable, strong upright chair: remember it has to take your weight and that of the instrument. If you are playing a blowing instrument such as the clarinet, oboe, trumpet or trombone, a mixture of mostly water from condensation and spit will drip either from the bell of the instrument, or in the case of the brass instruments, when you release the spit valve. The resulting drips come from a mixture of your saliva and the condensation of your breath on the cold inside of the instrument, and it is important to take steps to avoid dripping on to a light-coloured carpet or other soft furnishings. Some players simply put a tea towel or spare bit of carpet on the floor to deal with the problem.

The piano makes a sound easily, but other instruments provide a much greater challenge, and if you are finding it difficult to make and control your instrument's sounds as you wish to, it may help to pause and take stock. Most people when they become frustrated at not being able to do what they want to, become tense as well, and as their muscles tighten, they are actually increasing the likelihood of failure – so even though it is by far the hardest thing to do in this situation, the most vital key to success is to relax. Allow your mind to repeat the words that your teacher uses to help you make the sounds, and take plenty of short rests between your attempts. Less really is more in this situation, and when you do achieve success, take a break before trying again.

PRACTICAL TIPS FOR MAKING GOOD PROGRESS

If you have made a start with some lessons on your chosen instrument and you are finding it reasonably easy to play the notes that you need for your first pieces, it is time to explore some ideas to help you maintain that good progress. At this stage, learning may sometimes feel like two steps forwards and one step backwards, but that is to be expected because you are multi-tasking, and attempting to master a number of new skills all at the same time. Progress will, on occasion, be slower than you may wish it to be, but nevertheless it is progress.

Practising

Most adults look forward to practising because they are doing what they really want to do. They know that practice really is the key to success, and the idea of 'me time' that actually produces a beneficial and positive result is appealing, especially after a hard day at work. Practising can relieve tension that builds up so easily during the working day, it can occupy time if you're bored, and can easily produce a measurable result. Effective teachers will often invite students to play something they learned six weeks or six months ago to remind them of the progress that's been made, and you can always record yourself playing to monitor your own progress.

In his fascinating book *Not Pulling Strings* (Lambent Books, 1987), Joseph O'Connor writes about how he explored practice with his students, and he sums up their collective definition of practice as follows: 'It was repetitive, it isolated and concentrated on the difficult sections, it aimed at improvement and wasn't much fun.' Clearly, adult learners understand this, but there is no reason at all why any of us should feel like this about self-improvement – which is what practising is all about.

Finding the right time of day to practise can be tricky. It may be possible, if your chosen instrument is a portable one, to take it to work with you and to find a quiet place where you can do some playing at lunchtime. If your journey to work isn't too arduous, you may find time for some practice before setting off in the morning, and evenings and weekends should enable more valuable time to be put in. As with any form of learning, little and often is usually best, and for some instruments you may need to develop physical stamina, which a lack of, at the outset, will prevent you from playing for more than a few minutes.

The gaps between practising give your brain and muscle memory time to assimilate and consolidate what you are learning, making that time in between practices all the more important. This aspect of learning away from the instrument mirrors what has been developed in sports training. The old adage 'practice makes perfect' very easily becomes 'practice makes permanent', and if we do make something permanent we need to be sure it's absolutely right. This is where the weekly lesson with your teacher beats online learning and other forms of self-tuition, as the effective teacher can quickly put a simple error in posture, breathing or hand movement right, and save much wasted time later on.

Research has shown that most high-ranking professional musicians would practise for four to five hours a day at the most, finding that more than was simply counter productive. The majority also indicate that practising with the mind is as important as practising with the instrument. Dr K. Anders Ericsson's research has led him to put forward the view that it will take at least ten years, or ten thousand hours of practice, to achieve an expert level of performance in any subject area, and that for music it will be at least this much, and perhaps twice as long, to achieve elite performance level. For most adults this isn't a key issue, but if your progress does seem a little slower than you had hoped for, it may be worth keeping this in mind, especially when you feel like giving up.

Most adult learners don't encounter this issue in the same way that children and young people do. The adult learner has usually embarked on the learning journey after some careful thought and consideration. There may be the need to change to a different teacher or even to a different instrument, but your commitment will usually be there, unless for some reason it is squeezed out by poor teaching or unreasonable demands being made of you, or if your personal circumstances prevent sufficient time and energy to be given to the task in hand.

Choosing an Instrument
When it comes to choosing which instrument you want to play, the number of variables is so great that it is impossible to give one simple answer, but there are some straightforward practical matters you should consider:

- Your attitude to music itself and to instruments, and/or a specific instrument
- The sound of the instrument: we are often attracted to an instrument by its timbre. Some people just know what they want to play and they are usually right
- Your known, or estimated, musical aptitude and musical ability
- Teacher availability – access to lessons
- Who will provide your lessons: a music school or private teacher?
- The purchase or rental and subsequent running costs of your chosen instrument
- Your size and physical make-up
- The size and weight of your chosen instrument

One school of thought suggests that we should attempt to weigh up all the pros and cons of each instrument against all our identifiable characteristics in order to pick the instrument with which we are most likely to succeed in the long term. From a practical point of view this might be the ideal solution to avoid wasting time, money and effort all round. However, there is a risk that your chosen instrument is not the 'right' one for you, and that your decision has become a very 'left brain' one, rather than simply trusting your own feelings and intuition.

An alternative, and perhaps more pragmatic approach, is to work on the assumption that you may not carry on learning, or reach the highest levels of achievement. Most people will find it difficult to make a real choice about which instrument to start on. You should allow yourself to make several false starts, if you need to, over a period of time, and that way perhaps increase your chances of finding exactly the right instrument for you. After all, there is a fine balance between the journey and the destination: which is more important?

In Chapter 10 you will find plenty of information about most of the instruments found in the tradition of Western classical, jazz and popular music, but there is no substitute for allowing the music itself to influence your decision. Taking part through singing, for example, is an ideal starting point for many. Playing an instrument such as the recorder or ocarina, or some of the percussion family, provides an easy access route to ensemble music-making. Your gut reaction to hearing a musical ensemble playing live music could be the catalyst that makes you say 'I want to play one of those.' Initial exposure to as wide a range of music as possible will help you to form a judgement about what appeals to you most.

PRACTICAL ADVICE

Musician, composer and music educator Paul Harris often refers in his writings to the 'four Ps': posture, pulse, phonology (sound) and practice, emphasizing that these four aspects are the framework on which our music learning must be built. When you take time to consider how your music learning is progressing, it may be useful to start by thinking about those four aspects in particular.

In addition you might give some thought to more general and instrument-specific matters to help you with your learning, and to help you to develop as an all-round musician; these are also considered in this section.

Posture

With most instruments, starting to learn will involve adopting an unfamiliar posture in order to hold and make sounds on that instrument. An effective teacher can help with this by enabling you to focus on the most essential aspects, choosing to let some things go, knowing that they will be corrected in a few lessons' time. If you opt to learn online, it is probable that holding the instrument properly is likely to be the most difficult thing to master in the early stages. Use a mirror to check your posture as you practise, and check for any aches or pains or discomfort, and see if these relate to the way you are sitting or standing and holding your instrument. A partner or friend may be able to help you with this, but better still, set up your phone or tablet, and make a video clip of yourself playing. This way you can relate your tone production to your posture, and ensure that your instrument is being played in harmony with your body.

Another aspect of posture is the very act of carrying your instrument to a lesson. Even a light instrument, such as a flute, will pose some strain on the arm and back muscles if you have to carry it for any distance, and this effect is considerably increased when any larger instrument such as a trombone or cello is involved.

Pulse

We have already considered the terms pulse, beat and rhythm in Chapter 2. Establishing and maintaining a steady pulse is essential if you are to get the rhythm of a piece correct, and setting a slower tempo to begin with is almost always the best thing to do. As you gain fluency in a particular piece, remember to increase the tempo to the speed the composer has asked for. It may help to practise using a metronome, which could be mechanical, digital or app – but do so sparingly, otherwise your interpretation of the piece will be as mechanical as an old-fashioned, non-digital metronome used to be. The metronome is ideal for reminding you of the correct tempo before you play, or to help you to play scales or scale passages evenly.

In an ideal world it should be possible for you to play any piece at any tempo. The most common fault is settling on one speed and finding it difficult to play something at a different speed, be it more quickly or more slowly. Try to hear the piece or passage in your mind before you play it. Listen to it internally at different speeds, thinking of the arm, hand, finger or lip movements as you do so: that way you are not only preparing to play, but are also, in effect, practising as well.

Sound or Phonology

Playing music musically involves creating and controlling the sound of your instrument or voice. On woodwind and brasswind instruments you may find that the most effective exercises to improve your sound involve playing long-held notes at a variety of dynamics. The long notes help you to control the pressure with which you blow the air into the instrument, which is the key to success. It's a similar process with bowed string instruments, where the long notes help you to master bowing. As you become more able to listen critically to your own playing with real awareness, you can start to compare your own long notes one with another, working towards achieving complete consistency of tone, dynamics, attack, decay, and so on. As a general rule, practising a piece of music slowly is the best way towards being able to play it quickly.

Practice

At the start of this chapter some thoughts about practising were given. The key to success here lies in your concentration, and it is vital that you are listening carefully and attentively to what you're doing. As soon as the practice becomes simply repetition there is the risk that you play something incorrectly, and then learn it and remember it like that. There's a saying: 'Amateur players practise until they get it right; professionals practise until they can't play it wrongly.' You may have no thoughts about wanting to be a professional musician but the principle behind this saying is important, and it is well worth adopting that attitude. If you do, you will feel secure as a player, and when and if you choose to perform, that security will underpin your confidence as a performer.

Goal Setting

We live in a very goal-oriented world where target setting is viewed as the way of motivation for success. In businesses and schools the use of SMART goal-setting is often advocated: this acronym is simply a way of reminding us that goals should be specific, measurable, attainable, realistic and timely (sometimes the word tangible is substituted).

These principles can, of course, be applied to the work that we do on, and with, our voice or instrument between lessons. And there's no harm in having this in mind when preparing to tackle a new technical challenge, or to work on a longer piece of music. It is, however, crucial to remember that playing or singing music is not simply a question of getting things right or even perfect, because the most important thing we need to achieve is playing or singing music musically. If we bypass that in our approach, we do no more than produce a mechanistic result, which is definitely second best.

Breathing
Everyone expects that woodwind and brasswind players, and singers, will need to master certain aspects of breath control in order to produce a good sound. In fact, learning to breathe actively is a crucial part of the whole musical learning process, and is vitally important for all players, no matter what their instrument, and of course for singers. Something that we all do, involuntarily, is to hold our breath when we are trying to do something difficult, and this creates tension in the body, which in turn results in lack of muscle control – for example, when trying to play something you find difficult on a piano or stringed instrument. The little voice inside that says 'breathe' is a very important one.

One simple breathing exercise that anyone can do is to set a metronome to crotchet = 60 – that is, one beat per second – and having sat still for a minute or so, breathing normally, to move gradually to a breathing pattern where you have the same number of metronome beats for the inward breath as the outward breath. In this way you gradually take more notice of your breathing, and will begin to use you diaphragm muscles to control it. Revert to normal breathing at once if you feel any discomfort while doing this.

Concentration
It is, of course, important to be focused on the specific thing you are trying to do, but concentrating or trying too hard is generally counter productive. This leads to muscular tension and is linked directly to breathing. Whenever something is proving really difficult, just pause for a moment and focus on your breathing, rather than the task in hand. When you are practising at home it helps to eliminate as many distractions as possible, such as phones and other devices.

Vision
Make sure you can see what you're doing. If you are using sheet music, make sure it is at the right height for you, is well lit, and that you don't need to lean towards it to see the notation when you're playing. When you play with other musicians in a small or large ensemble you will need to catch sight of other players and the conductor, if there is one. You will acquire the skill of being able to keep an eye on the music, note what your fellow players are doing and watch the conductor, all at the same time. It comes with practice and experience.

It is also worth mentioning the attribute known as proprioception at this point, as it is something that musicians use quite a lot. Experienced pianists use it when they need to play a note at an extreme point on the keyboard from where their hands have been. A combination of visual and other sensory information enables them to locate that distant note without too much difficulty, whereas the less experienced player would need much more visual information to do this reliably. String players similarly need to know where to place their fingers on the fingerboard to produce the next note, and do so using little, if any, visual information. It is also proprioception that enables musicians to start a piece or a phrase of music together without apparently giving one another any signals. In fact the signals are there, but are often so tiny as to be invisible to anyone other than those sitting very close by.

TIPS FOR PLAYING AND SINGING MUSICALLY

It is, of course, much easier to play or sing music badly, rather than playing it well. Yet if you ask people about this, very few would say that they were intending to play badly. So what is it that makes the difference? Playing or singing the notes correctly is the first part of developing a musical performance, but strangely, it isn't necessarily the most important part. Of course, the right notes do matter, but it is the way the notes are created and controlled, and joined together to make phrases, which builds a musical performance that can convey meaning and emotion to the listener.

It is easier to define unmusical or non-musical playing first. Simply listen to a computer program playing a composition to you, and you should hear all the correct notes, rhythms and perhaps some dynamics, all played with a steady pulse – but it is unlikely to sound musical. The reason for this is that, at a basic level, software cannot provide the nuances that a human performer does, and it is the nuance in the way these sounds are begun, shaped and sustained, and how they decay, that we begin to feel and glimpse musical playing. Slight variations in speed against a steady pulse and dynamics that suit the context of the performance all contribute to the idea of playing music musically.

Music is often referred to as an international language, and this is true inasmuch as it is a non-verbal language where the nuances of attack, sustain and decay on each individual sound and groups of sounds together, combine to give it form and meaning. Keeping this in mind is just as important as struggling to get the notes right.

Taking a step back to listen, perhaps to a recording of yourself, will always be instructive.

Listening Skills

Becoming an active listener is a crucial component of learning to play or sing musically, and you need to move from simply hearing the sound to actively listening to it. Did you play the right note at the right time in the right place with the appropriate degree of attack, and at a suitable dynamic? Was your intonation good – in other words, were the notes you played in tune? With the exception of the piano, you may need to adjust tuning, or intonation, of every note. If you're playing music with other people, you may need to tune your note to theirs, not just to the exact pitch of a tuning fork or electronic tuner. Were all the notes you played shaped into a phrase? Did the musical sounds you created convey something to a listener, real or imaginary?

One of the easiest ways to improve your listening skills is to take simple tunes that you already know and find them on your instrument. These should be tunes that you can sing or whistle fairly confidently, so that someone listening to you sing or whistle them can recognize the melody. Essentially, by doing this you are learning to play by ear, and even though this may not be one of your goals in learning to play a musical instrument, it is a really effective way of focusing how you listen.

Similarly, listening to music being played whilst following the notation is a very good discipline, and will also help you to develop your aural skills. It is hard to be an active listener when much of your effort may be centred on simply producing the sounds. Take a break from practice by listening to other musicians, recorded or live, to increase your aural and musical acuity. Listening to music that is unfamiliar, perhaps in a style or genre that you have not explored before, is also beneficial in terms of developing your listening skills.

TIPS FOR DIFFERENT INSTRUMENTS

Bowed Stringed Instruments

Bowed stringed instruments include the violin, viola, cello and double bass, and as soon as you feel confident to check your instrument's tuning you will be in a better position to get a good sound, because it will produce a better and much more satisfying tone when it is in tune. You may have an electronic tuner, which is good to use sometimes, but you will find that training your ear, rather than relying on your eyes watching the device, will, in the long run, be much more fruitful.

Posture is of vital importance to ensure that you have free movement of both your bowing arm and your fingers on the strings. You are adopting an unnatural position to play your instrument, so be alert for tensions creeping in, as these can easily lead to discomfort. You can rehearse your standing or sitting position with an imaginary instrument, and use this for checking where the tensions arise. Similarly, being able to think of your left-hand fingers on the fingerboard, and visualizing which sound they would be making, is a really good way of consolidating what you are learning in the early stages. Singing the note you want to play is highly beneficial, and singing the bar, phrase or piece will help. Hearing the sounds before you play them helps with pitch, intonation and rhythm.

Time spent on bow speed, bow position and the distance of the bow from the bridge will bring the biggest rewards in terms of developing your sound. At the outset you may find that the sound you are making is a long way removed from the sound you have heard a professional player produce, and which perhaps inspired you to take up the instrument. But it is important to remember that, with very rare exceptions, all string players have been through this stage, and also to bear in mind that the sooner you can join some form of ensemble, the better it will be, as a large group of strings playing together will nearly always sound better at this stage.

Plucked Stringed Instruments

Plucked stringed instruments include the harp, the acoustic guitar, electric guitar, electric bass, mandolin, ukelele, balalaika and banjo.

Playing the guitar, mandolin, ukelele, balalaika or banjo can easily mean that you adopt a very hunched sitting position, which may result in tension and discomfort. With all these instruments it is very easy to tense muscles, as your mind is likely to associate this with the notion of 'trying'. If you can detach your thinking from the action you are taking, it will become easier to produce the sounds that you really want.

You will need to develop the skill of knowing where your left hand is on the fretboard so that you can rely on feeling your fingering position, to some extent, rather than relying totally on visually checking it. This is often referred to as 'finger memory'. The same principle regarding positioning applies to playing the harp (see Proprioception above).

When you are practising finger position or chord changes on any of these instruments, slow it down, so that instead of changing from one beat to the next you put in an empty beat in which to check your fingers before playing. That way you will only hear the right sound when you make it. If you change quickly and hear the wrong sound, that is what you will remember, and so you are practising playing the music incorrectly, which is clearly not a good thing to do.

Brass Instruments

Brass instruments include the cornet, trumpet, flugelhorn, tenor horn, baritone horn, French horn, trombone, euphonium and sousaphone.

The key to success with these instruments lies in developing your lip flexibility and the strength in the huge number of small muscles around your mouth, to ensure that you can create the sound and pitch that you want. You also need to be sure that the valves on these instruments, or slide on the trombone, are working efficiently: your teacher will be able to advise you about this, and in the early stages of learning it is better not to take the valves apart without the teacher's guidance.

The combination of your blowing and your instrument's mechanics will enable you to produce the sounds you want, but of course this can only be achieved if you are simultaneously developing your aural perception. In other words, your ear needs to recognize that you've hit the right note or made the right sound, or to inform you that the note or sound you've made is too high or too low so that next time you can make the appropriate embouchure adjustment.

Remember to check from time to time that the instrument's tubing is clear of water. If you are sitting down, sit forward on the chair with your feet flat on the floor. After two or three months' playing, your instrument will need to be taken to pieces and cleaned, and it is best to let your teacher help you with this until you feel confident to do it by yourself.

Woodwind Instruments

Woodwind instruments include the flute, oboe, clarinet, bassoon and saxophone. They depend on a combination of your fingers covering the holes or pressing the keys, and efficient keywork, to make them play and sound the notes easily. Your teacher should be able to check this for you, and may be able to carry out simple repairs if necessary. The instruments with reeds, whether single as in the clarinet and saxophone, or double in the oboe and bassoon, also need a good reed that is right for you and the instrument. As a beginner it is difficult to choose a reed for yourself, but your teacher will help, and you will very soon find that you are able to discriminate between 'good' reeds and 'bad' ones. If your reed doesn't help you to make the sound easily, check with your teacher to see if there is anything you can do to improve matters. This might be quite simple – for example, pressing a clarinet reed firmly with your thumb can help to make it a little easier to blow. For clarinets and saxophones, a soft reed, numbered 1½ to 2, is usually best for beginners.

Playing long notes and keeping the sound and pitch steady may be a little boring, but this sort of practice will pay huge dividends through helping you to really control sound and tone production. Corked joints need to fit snugly, and again, your teacher should be able to help or advise with this. Regular maintenance of these mechanical aspects is crucial to your success as a player. As with the instruments of the brass family, a lot also depends on your embouchure and the musculature around your mouth, which will take time to develop.

Keyboard Instruments

Keyboard instruments include the piano, organ and harpsichord.

Good posture is vital when playing at a keyboard, and an adjustable stool will enable you to ensure that your arms and hands are at the right height, with your fingers in the right position for the keyboard. If your stool isn't adjustable, use cushions or books to make your sitting position higher if necessary.

Once you can remember a piece, try playing it with your eyes closed to improve your fingers' understanding of where the keys are, and to help you concentrate purely on the sounds, rather than the notation and then the sounds. As you don't have to make an effort to create the sound, try picking out tunes that you know: this is an excellent aural development exercise, and as your confidence grows you will be able to add some simple left-hand chords to accompany the melody. It's a good idea to play with your eyes closed, as this will help your knowledge of keyboard geography and will reduce your dependency on looking at notation.

If you develop any tension in your arms, shoulders or legs you will need to adjust your sitting position. A good teacher will help you to get this right.

Electronic Instruments

Electronic instruments include the electronic piano, synthesizer, or other electronic keyboards, and the electric and bass guitars.

If you are learning any electronic instrument, the first thing to check is that electrically it is safe in itself, and that there is no risk to you, or anyone else, of tripping over a stray electronic lead. You should exercise special caution when buying a secondhand electronic instrument or amplifier.

The touch on an electronic keyboard is different to that of an acoustic piano, and different sorts of electronic keyboard or electric piano have different features associated with the touch. If you are having piano lessons but use an electronic instrument at home to practise on, be sure to inform your piano teacher so they can make allowance for this.

In terms of learning to play a keyboard, the remarks for piano or guitar above also apply. The great advantage with all these instruments is that you can play them without making any sound other than through your headphones, so they may be ideal if you choose not to disturb others, or live in a flat or a property where you know the sound will carry and cause a nuisance.

Percussion Instruments

Percussion instruments include drums, the marimba, glockenspiel and timpani, orchestral percussion, and others.

Non-pitched percussion instruments can be frustrating to practise on their own, so try using a recorded backing of some sort while playing on headphones, as this can help you to retain focus during practice sessions. You can do all your percussion learning electronically so that you don't disturb others, but if you want to play music with other people you will also have to get used to using acoustic instruments.

Using electronic support is also a good way of keeping the pulse steady, and percussionists often have to do this for the band or ensemble in which they are playing. Counting out loud helps develop pulse too, and you can record yourself to check if this is working for you.

Posture and playing position are just as important for percussion as for any other instrument. To play the drums you need to have free independent movement of your arms, hands, legs and feet, so balance will also be a key feature.

TIPS FOR SINGERS

Part of the problem for singers is that the 'instrument' producing the sound isn't visible. Some singing teachers work using metaphor to describe the sensations that you will explore as a singer, while others use a more factual approach, seeking to ensure that you are aware of all the relevant parts of your body that are involved. Both approaches can work equally well, so seek out a teacher who uses whichever one works best for you to ensure that you understand what to do in order to adjust and develop the sound you are making. Posture and breathing are crucial components of successful singing, and learning to breathe with your diaphragm is vitally important. One way to practise breathing is to lie flat on your back on the floor with your hands on your stomach: breathe in and your hands will rise; then breathe out and they will lower. This means you are breathing correctly, and you should try to do this when you are singing.

In fact this exercise is beneficial for all instruments, even ones that do not involve blowing, because it helps to establish effective breathing, thus releasing tension for whatever you are attempting to do.

CHAPTER 9

Personal Stories

By reading this book you have chosen to seek some advice, and get some information at your fingertips, before starting to learn a musical instrument or resuming your studies. What could be better than hearing from some adults who have done just this? While not all of the following accounts have completely happy endings, there are things to be learned from them. For example, are you keen to take music exams – would they help to motivate you? There are five accounts of learning experiences; the adults in the first two accounts both learnt the piano, but the outcome for each was quite different, and they had rather different experiences on their musical journeys.

PAUL'S STORY

Let's start with Paul's story. Paul is now in his late thirties and runs a very successful one-man business, with a work diary that is always booked for up to six months ahead. He says that music at school didn't make much impact on him, but there was family involvement in music-making, particularly through participation at church. Whilst at middle school, when he was about twelve years of age, Paul started to learn the guitar. He was motivated to do this through his enjoyment of two quite contrasting styles of music: on the one hand the music of Dire Straits and in particular guitarist Eric Clapton, and on the other, the performances of Michael Card, an American Christian singer-songwriter, musician, author and radio host.

It's not unusual to enjoy listening to differing sorts of music, nor to want to play in both styles, although many people might say they were discouraged from listening to one sort of music or another. Although he had some guitar lessons, Paul really made progress with his playing through listening over and over again to passages of the music he liked, and gradually finding out how to make those sounds on his guitar. It wasn't until some years later that he realized that many of the pieces he had wanted to play were really beyond the technical ability he had at the time, but such was his enthusiasm for playing that he persevered until he could play what he wanted to. He had little or no interest in classical music at this time.

A few years later, when he was about sixteen, he began piano lessons, continuing with tuition until he was about twenty. This tuition was focused on the traditional classical repertoire. During all this time, the principal outlet for Paul's developing musical prowess was joining in with, and playing, music at church. Then in his early twenties Paul moved away from his music-making for a number of years. This may have been part of the process of moving into adulthood, establishing a career, and getting married when he was twenty-five.

In his late twenties he was drawn back to music and resumed piano lessons. By now his musical outlook had changed, and although he still enjoyed popular music he was increasingly drawn to the classical repertoire and had discovered the Beethoven piano sonatas, and pieces by Chopin, which especially appealed to him. He decided to take grade five, which he passed with a high merit, but describes the day of the exam in this way: 'It made me feel ill and very anxious. Once I started playing, though, it was all right, and the examiner did everything to put me at my ease.' The idea of taking exams was prompted partly by the fact that, looking ahead, Paul was contemplating the possibility of working perhaps part-time as a music teacher, and he felt that it would be important for him to be able to show learners, or their parents, that he had some qualifications.

Paul no longer has lessons, but plays the piano and guitar regularly at his church. He has found that learning to play the guitar has given him a good understanding of chords, which in turn enables him to play music in a popular style on the piano from chord symbols and a melody line. This gives him a huge advantage in terms of not always needing fully notated music, and whilst playing, being able to look away from the music to his fellow musicians more easily. This increases his enjoyment of making music with other people, which is important for him.

Having reached a standard where he can make music confidently with other people, Paul knows that his ability to play music will always be there, and that he can return to music-making whenever he chooses.

ELIZABETH'S STORY

Our second learner is Elizabeth. She enjoyed her convent primary school, although she was less happy at the state secondary school she attended. She sang in both the school choir and another local one, not connected to the school. Her parents decided she should learn the piano, and by the age of eight or nine Elizabeth wanted to learn the flute. But her parents told her that she could only learn one instrument, and it didn't occur to Elizabeth to give up her piano lessons; so she never had flute lessons whilst at school, and continued with the piano, which she didn't particularly enjoy. She found her piano teacher unsympathetic, and lessons consisted primarily of preparation for the next graded exam; she says, 'I learnt three pieces a year just to pass the next exam.' She passed grade five at her second attempt, at the age of sixteen, and then stopped all musical activity. She felt her piano learning had been rote based, and although she could play the notes and achieve exam success, she felt that she didn't really understand music.

When Elizabeth left school she took a business studies course at a polytechnic, which meant moving quite a long way from home. Whilst there, she continued to go out with a boy she had been going out with at school, and was engaged by the time she took her finals. Interestingly, Elizabeth chose a grand piano as a wedding present.

At the age of twenty-three she found an old clarinet in the family and began playing. She tried several teachers, and despite some dissatisfaction with various individuals, made good progress, although it took until she was in her late thirties before she passed her grade eight. Elizabeth had three children in fairly rapid succession while still in her twenties, and she felt that several of her clarinet teachers didn't accept that the pressures of being a young mother often prevented her from practising as much as she would have liked to.

She had focused on human resources at degree level and had developed a successful career in this field, but having children of her own made her want to shift from HR to music, and she gradually moved her working life into music teaching. Now, with two of her children in higher education and the youngest coming to the end of his schooldays, a significant part of her life involves music and music-making. The other arts are much less important to Elizabeth. All three of her children are actively involved in music, and one of them is studying music at a university.

Elizabeth feels that adult learners are mostly very dedicated, but often need nurturing. She can base this view on both her own experiences and the adults she now teaches. For example, she told me that 'taking an exam as an adult can be very hard. You are often in a waiting room with children who are making more rapid progress than you are – you could even be taking an exam at the same time as your own children.' Elizabeth also feels that while there are many music-making opportunities for children provided by schools and other local amateur groups, similar opportunities for adults may be harder to find, and an adult may not to wish to join an ensemble where most of the group is made up of teenagers.

Now in her late forties, Elizabeth enjoys her work as a music teacher and feels she teaches adults effectively because she has a greater empathy with them, having in many respects been a late starter in music herself. All her musical education has been self-funded, and this has included continuing professional development courses to further her skills as a teacher and musician. Despite many years of hard work, she has an inner frustration that she is not always able to attain the standards she aspires to. While all three of her children have had regular lessons and have been able to make rapid progress, Elizabeth can't always afford to do this for herself, nor find the time to practise as much as she would like to.

Once again, Elizabeth's story raises the question of music exams. There is more about the graded structure of music exams in Chapter 3.

COLIN'S STORY

Colin's story is perhaps less typical. Colin's father played the piano and had achieved grade eight by the age of sixteen. Colin became involved in music at church, and although he was given the opportunity to learn a musical instrument, no pressure was applied to make him do so. He tried the violin when he was about seven or eight, but didn't feel at ease with his teacher, so gave up and started piano at the age of eleven. He had lessons for a few years, occasionally played the hymns for church, and passed grade two when he was about twelve, although he chose not to take any more exams. He sang in the choir at secondary school, and his father encouraged him to take an 'O'-level music course, although in the end he didn't actually take the exam. Colin's music-making mostly took place outside school, and a lot of it was connected with his church.

At around the age of fifteen he taught himself to strum chords on the guitar. After taking his 'A' levels he went to work, and soon got married; he continued playing the piano, but without making any 'new' progress. While at university he made some enquiries about learning the harp, but this didn't come to anything. However, his wife was musical: she had played percussion at school, and had also had piano and guitar lessons.

Some years later Colin had a young family, and felt that learning an instrument might be good for his young son, whom he thought would gain greater confidence from participation in music. One of Colin's university students suggested he try the local brass band, and when he took his son along to an evening practice, he was immediately struck by how friendly and supportive the whole community was. His son was loaned an instrument and given free tuition, and this prompted Colin to join in as well! He started on the cornet but moved quickly to baritone, then later to trombone. It was clear that the trombone was the right instrument for Colin. A year later his daughter also joined the training band. Soon after this, although not in any way because of it, his son left the brass band and took up the piano.

Colin's daughter made rapid progress, and quickly moved from the training band to the main band, where she was soon playing on the front row in the cornet section, 'second man down' from the section principal. Colin also moved to the main band, where he played trombone, bass trombone or percussion, depending on requirements and the balance of available players. Now in his mid-forties he has recently become the musical director of the training band, a role that he relishes.

It is clear from Colin's story that music has always been important to him, but he feels that until joining the local brass band he never found quite the right outlet for his passion, and it wasn't until he started playing the trombone that he found 'his' instrument.

TINA'S STORY

Our next story is quite unusual, and involves an instrument that is very much in the minority when it comes to the number of learners and performers who play it.

Tina attended mainstream school and hated music lessons. She found notation difficult, and still feels that she hasn't really mastered it. She doesn't remember singing whilst at school, and describes herself as tone deaf. Neither of her parents showed any musical prowess, although her younger brother and sister did pursue musical interests, her sister playing the flute and later the violin, and her brother the drums.

Tina left school and went to work. Some years later she took a course in counselling, and a fellow student recommended that she should go for an energy field healing treatment. In Tina's words: 'This significantly changed my perspective on life.' About a week after she began a course of therapy she felt that she wanted to play the harp, searched the internet for a local teacher, and went for her first lesson. Now, some three years later, she continues to love everything about the instrument, despite describing the process of learning to play it as 'a struggle'.

Tina's harp teacher has encouraged her to take exams if she chooses to, and she has now passed grades one and two and is working towards taking her grade three. Coincidentally, Tina's mother has now begun keyboard lessons, and they enjoy discussing their achievements and frustrations with the learning process when they get together.

Tina's advice to a would-be learner on any instrument is simple and direct: 'Just do it!' For her, there is no doubt that the harp is the right instrument. 'I'm drawn to it,' she says, 'and it makes me feel good just looking at it and touching it.' Tina has no aspirations to playing the harp in an orchestra, nor is she particularly interested in making music with other people. 'Maybe one day I'll be good enough to play for weddings!'

It's clear that for Tina, who is in her early forties, music is mostly a solitary occupation. She didn't choose to learn an instrument to enhance her social life, but it has filled a void that is perhaps somewhere on the spectrum of spirituality and culture.

CHRISTINE'S STORY

Finally, let's meet Christine, for whom music has played an important part in her life since her primary school days. Both her parents were musical: her mother played the piano, and her father sang. Christine began piano lessons at the age of seven, opting to study the piano rather than go to ballet classes. She continued lessons until she took her school exams at the age of sixteen, reaching about grade four in standard. She was never particularly comfortable at performing, but enjoyed playing and became quite a proficient sight-reader. She also played percussion in the Girls' Brigade band, and was often involved in music-making through her church.

When she left school she studied optometry at City University in London. During the period from starting university to sometime after she married in her late twenties, music faded very much into the background. However, things changed when her husband bought her a piano, and she then resumed lessons, continuing with them intermittently for a further eighteen years. At this point she attended a wedding where there was a harpist playing at the reception. This really captured her imagination, and as a fifty-ninth birthday present she booked herself a lesson on the harp. This captivated her, and she continued with lessons intermittently for some eighteen months without having her own instrument to practise on – and then she decided to take the plunge, buy a harp, and be rather more serious about the whole process.

Since then she hasn't looked back, and some three years later says that when she plays the harp she enters another world, which she just loves. It was being close to the instrument and hearing it played live that really sparked her initial interest. In her early sixties, Christine's motivation to continue is that of learning to play particular melodies she is especially fond of: 'I play for my own pleasure, and I'm not looking for an audience.'

From both of the harp stories it is clear that there really is something about the instrument which makes it feel as if the harp itself chooses the learner, as much as the other way round.

IN SUMMARY

The stories related here are all true, and serve to give a flavour of the experiences of some individuals. Your story may be similar, but is just as likely to be completely different, and it's best just to see them as a point of reference, rather than allowing them to guide you in one direction or another.

CHAPTER 10

Detailed Information on Singing and Instruments

This chapter starts by taking a look at singing, for one very simple reason: it is the cheapest and most readily available option for the vast majority of adults who would like to take part in some music-making. Then more detailed information is given about different instruments.

SINGING

Singing is an excellent way to develop aural perception and this lies at the heart of all music-making. As a child or young person you should have had the opportunity to sing at school, either with your classmates as part of the music curriculum, or by joining a choir. You may have sung in a religious context, in a secular one such as at a football match or on the coach returning from a day trip, but it is an encounter that should have happened to you. There may, however, be many reasons why this didn't happen, or why you were reluctant to take part, and now could be just the time to put all that behind you.

There is no doubt that taking part in choral activity is beneficial both as a precursor and as an adjunct to instrumental lessons. Singing may help you with breathing, posture, self-esteem, aural awareness, pulse and rhythm, amongst other things. It's a very good way into musical activity, with little or no initial cost involved. Many towns and villages will have some sort of choral group that is open to anyone to join without any form of test or audition. For as many people who are attracted by joining such a local choral group, an equal number will be put off by the thought of singing music they don't feel a connection with. Fortunately, in recent years there has been a growth of organizations such as 'Rock choir', which offers a locally based singing experience performing contemporary popular music. Again, there is no audition requirement, and participants have the opportunity to perform at both a local and national level.

Adult voices are usually categorized as soprano, contralto (usually known as alto), tenor, baritone and bass. Soprano and alto are the female voices, with soprano having the higher range of the two. Similarly with men's voices, the tenor is the highest and baritone is the middle range. There are further subdivisions such as mezzo soprano, literally half soprano, with its range being between soprano and alto. The term 'treble' voice is usually applied to children's voices, boys and girls, and specifically to boys before their voices break. The change of register or vocal range that occurs at puberty doesn't mean that men have no high notes at all, but it does mean that in order to sing in this high range they will need to sing in their falsetto register. That falsetto voice is then known as counter tenor, which is a classical male voice that uses the same range as the female contralto or mezzo soprano. It was in common usage in times gone by when women did not sing in choirs. It is used today in cathedral or church choirs, by male vocalists specializing in early music, and also in pop music.

You may not know what your voice is, and it doesn't matter at all. If you join any sort of choir or singing group the musical director should be able to help you find the right part to sing, which will suit your vocal capabilities. In the same way that it is possible to learn to play the cornet or trumpet by joining a brass band, you can learn to sing, read music and sing a particular part by joining a choir or choral group. If you want to take it further you could also have singing lessons, but it's not essential to do that just to get started. If you're worried that you already know that you find it difficult to hold a tune or get the pitches of notes right, have a word with the musical director of your chosen group first. It would be a good idea to go along and listen to part of a rehearsal, to see if you enjoy the sorts of music the group is singing. You could also purchase an app to help develop your pitching skills.

Singing lessons from a good teacher will help you to focus your sound, develop your understanding of breathing for singing, to pitch notes consistently in tune, and to tackle an appropriate repertoire for your developing voice. As with most instruments, there are apps available that will support your learning, but there is no substitute for a teacher working with you in the same room. The human voice is a sensitive instrument and quite easily damaged. If you drop your trombone on the floor it is simply a matter of finding the money to repair or replace it, but if you damage your vocal folds, you may cause permanent damage or require significant medical treatment to put them right.

Singing is sometimes described as a form of sustained speech, and essentially your voice is characterized by the way you use your lungs, by the cavities in your head which act as resonators, and by your larynx and your tongue, palate, teeth and lips, which enable you to articulate the sounds that you are singing. Your voice will have a number of natural registers, and by developing it, as a singer, you will be able to strengthen certain registers to give you your own individual vocal sound. With training and practice you will learn to project your voice, and gain volume, depth and character.

On the Heart Research website there is a quote from Professor Graham Welch, Chair of Music Education at the Institute of Education, University of London, who has studied developmental and medical aspects of singing for thirty years. He says that the health benefits of singing are both physical and psychological:

> Singing has physical benefits because it is an aerobic activity that increases oxygenation in the bloodstream and exercises major muscle groups in the upper body, even when sitting. Singing has psychological benefits because of its normally positive effect in reducing stress levels through the action of the endocrine system, which is linked to our sense of emotional well-being. Psychological benefits are also evident when people sing together as well as alone because of the increased sense of community, belonging and shared endeavour.

Like all musical activities, singing benefits from practice. The voice is a muscle and will benefit from exercise – though gently at first, of course. The great thing about singing is that you can practise almost anywhere, and if you drive a car, that's an ideal place to make as much noise as you like, if you are on your own!

INTRODUCTION TO INSTRUMENTS

In this part of the book you'll find some detailed information about most instruments, to help you make your decision about which one to begin learning. It's impossible to include every instrument from which you could choose, but the most popular ones for beginners, or those continuing their instrumental music learning, are included here. If you are starting from scratch, you may find it useful to read about a number of instruments and compare the pros and cons of purchasing, looking after and maintaining each of them, to help you make up your mind.

Evidence regarding the popularity of instruments comes in part from sales figures, and also from the number of candidates entered for graded music exams. It will probably come as no surprise to find that the piano is at the head of the list, followed by violin, flute, clarinet and trumpet. However, that need not influence your decision, which should be based on a combination of personal preference and being practical about your choice.

Here is a final set of questions to help you make up your mind as to which instrument to choose, or whether to opt for singing:

- Do you see/feel/hear yourself playing an instrument from a particular family: strings, woodwind, brasswind, percussion, keyboard?
- Do you see/feel/hear yourself playing music in a particular style or genre?
- How important is the size and portability of the instrument?
- How important is the volume level you might make practising at home?
- Do you have a particular musical goal in mind, such as playing in the local brass band, playing in the local amateur orchestra, playing jazz in a pub, playing cocktail lounge piano, being a member of a string quartet?
- If you are giving 'don't know' answers to these questions, have you decided between an instrument and singing?
- Have you thought seriously about joining a singing group to try out music-making, with the option to move to an instrument whenever you choose?

STRINGED INSTRUMENTS

L–R: Two violins, viola and cello.

Cello.

The complete string family today includes instruments with a very long history, such as the harp, and those with a much shorter one, such as the electric guitar. Stringed instruments divide into two main categories: those that are exclusively plucked and mostly have metal strips called frets across the fingerboard; and those that make their sound by having a bow drawn across the strings, in addition to making sounds by being plucked. The harp is the exception, where the strings are plucked and there is no bow, no fingerboard and no frets.

The orchestral strings include the violin, viola (pronounced vee-o luh), 'cello (pronounced 'chello', and its full name is violoncello) and double bass; all have a similar body shape, and a design that has changed little since their original development in the early seventeenth century. The instruments themselves are made of wood and held together entirely by glue. The bow is made of wood with horsehair, or a modern synthetic fibre, which is stretched and tightened by means of a long screw. All four instruments each have four strings, tuned to G-D-A-E on the violin, C-G-D-A on the viola and 'cello, and E-A-D-G on the double bass. All four instruments can play an extensive chromatic range of notes, and in the symphony orchestra are played as part of a section which could include as many as twenty-four violins, divided into two parts, first and seconds, eight violas, twelve 'cellos and eight double basses. While European makers dominate the high end of the market, their place has been taken in recent years by instruments manufactured in eastern Europe and China, which though once considered only good enough for the beginner end of the market, are gaining ground, in terms of quality, at a formidable rate.

The guitar is the commonest of the plucked stringed instruments, and can be played in a folk style, usually strumming chords, or 'picked' to play single notes, or as a classical instrument. It has six strings tuned E-A-D-G-B-E, and the strings are plucked with the

Double bass.

fingers or using a small piece of plastic, held between the finger and thumb, called a plectrum. The guitar's electric counterpart is played in a similar fashion and often provides a chordal backing or lead melody or a mixture of both. The bass guitar with its four strings provides the bass line in the same way as the double bass does in an orchestra.

The mandolin and banjo are rarely taught in schools, but the ukelele has become a popular choice for beginners in the past few years. If one of these instruments captures your imagination, it is always worth asking a guitar teacher, as they may double on one or more of them, and if not, are quite likely to know of any local player-teachers.

The harp is the oldest member of the string family and is found in two forms today: the smaller folk harp or clarsach (Gaelic for 'small harp'), and the orchestral harp. The clarsach is more readily portable and quieter in tone than the orchestral harp, which is more difficult to transport.

String players often seem to be the slightly more serious members of an orchestra. They need to look after their quite fragile instruments, maintain the bow and deal with tuning. Playing a stringed instrument requires sophisticated co-ordination, perseverance, and good aural perception, or the ability to hear a note 'internally' before playing it. The absence of frets on the fingerboard means that players need to learn where the notes are, whereas their guitarist counterparts are provided with an indication of where to place their fingers.

Learning to play the violin, viola, 'cello or double bass takes a good deal of time, patience and perseverance, but an accomplished player will gain access to some of the world's most beautiful music, and an enormous quantity of music has been composed for these instruments. Many violinists go on playing and performing to a very advanced age.

BOWED STRINGED INSTRUMENTS

Bowed strings include the violin, viola, 'cello and double bass.

Violin

The violin has the largest repertoire of all Western classical instruments, other than the piano. Most violinists will play as part of an ensemble, and music for the violin includes ensemble and orchestral compositions from the late Baroque period through the Classical and Romantic eras to the present day. The violin features as a solo instrument in the concertos of Bach, Beethoven, Berg, Brahms, Bruch, Elgar, Mozart, Mendelssohn, Sibelius, Tchaikovsky and many other composers. It can be played in a string quartet, which consists of two violins, a viola and a 'cello, and the instrument features in light and popular music of the mid- and late twentieth century. It was played in jazz ensembles such as the quintet of the Hot Club of France, by Stéphane Grapelli, and continues to feature as a jazz instrument, for example as played by Nigel Kennedy. There is a lot of music written for violin and piano.

The instrument itself is largely unchanged since its development in the late sixteenth century, and to this day, instruments from this period, especially those made by Stradivari, Guarneri and Amati, are the most sought after by both collectors and performers. Violins are made in a range of sizes to suit the size of the player. The sounds are made by drawing a bow, usually held in the right hand, across the strings of the instrument, or on some occasions, plucking the strings with the right hand. The difficulty of bowing is exacerbated by the fact that the instrument is positioned under the left chin, too close to be looked at comfortably and clearly. Playing the violin requires simultaneous independent activity with each hand, something that some learners may find difficult.

Teaching methods such as Suzuki focus on tone production, aural development and memorization, with less emphasis placed initially on written notation and learning to read music. As with any instrument, the quality of teaching is paramount, regardless of the particular method adopted. Ensemble activity has been shown as the most likely to motivate beginner violinists, and so an opportunity to play with a group, perhaps in the evening or at weekends, is important. Learning to play the violin requires patience and perseverance on the part of the player. You may start by simply plucking the strings to get used to the posture that you need to play the instrument, and then move to making sounds with the bow. In the hands of a beginner, the violin will make a sound that many people will find less than attractive, for some time. Good hand-eye co-ordination is important.

The purchase price for a first instrument is modest, but as the quality improves, so does the price, and dramatically so! There is a plentiful supply of secondhand instruments, although many learners prefer to buy a new one. Running costs for the violin are minimal. You can expect to buy replacement strings, as these can break when stretched through over-enthusiastic tuning, or may simply wear out. Bows need to be re-haired from time to time, and have an adjustment mechanism that may require occasional maintenance. The violin is sensitive to rough handling and changes in temperature, so should be stored away from direct sunlight or sources of heat.

Viola

The viola, pronounced vee-o luh, is now commonly taught as a beginner's instrument. Many adult violinists also play and teach the viola. In much orchestral music the viola plays an important but sometimes less musically interesting rôle, providing neither the glamour nor drama of the melody, nor the strength of the bass line. Perhaps it is for this reason that both the instrument and sometimes the player have become the butt of many musicians' jokes.

Its rôle in the orchestra is a vital one, and great composers such as Mozart were viola players, along with Haydn and Beethoven. A number of fine works have been written for it, including concertos by two great English composers, Sir Malcolm Arnold and Sir William Walton. Playing the viola almost certainly means playing in a symphony orchestra, a string orchestra or a string quartet, and in the longer term, a violist will play the repertoire associated with these ensembles.

The viola is held, like the violin, under the left side of the chin, and the player 'stops' or presses the strings on to the fingerboard with the left hand to change the pitch of the notes, while making the sound with the right hand either by plucking the strings or drawing a bow across them.

It is quite possible to play music written for the viola on a violin strung and tuned as a viola, and in a school where a number of children are learning stringed instruments, the teacher may do this as a way of introducing children to the instrument, thus providing an intermediate step in the process of transferring from violin to viola. Some violins are now especially adapted with a 'hole' drilled in the front which has made for a much better quality viola sound. In terms of music written which includes the viola, and the processes associated with learning, these are all similar to the violin. However, notation for the viola does not use the more familiar treble clef but is written in the viola or alto clef, which must also be learnt. Learning to play the viola affords the same opportunities and challenges as learning to play the violin, and good hand-eye co-ordination is similarly very important.

The purchase price of a viola is modest, and secondhand instruments are quite readily available. Many students prefer to buy a new one, but as usual, follow the advice of your teacher. As with the violin, the running costs are minimal, replacement strings being the main factor, with occasional re-hairing of the bow.

Like the violin, violas are also made in smaller sizes to accommodate smaller players, but those learners who move to the viola from the violin are less likely to do so until they are playing on the full size instrument. Although a little heavier than the violin, the viola is a very manageable and easily portable instrument. As a viola player you are likely to find a warm welcome in most amateur ensembles as there is something of a shortage of players.

Violoncello, or Cello

The 'cello (its usual name, although its full name is violoncello) is quite a fragile instrument, and even the smaller sized versions are quite bulky to carry around. It provides the lowest notes in a string quartet and produces a sound that many learners, adults and children, find appealing, especially as the instrument rests against the player which means that you really feel, as well as hear, the notes.

Again, as with the violin, playing the 'cello almost certainly means playing in a symphony orchestra, a string orchestra or a string quartet. The 'cello repertoire is huge and is principally of music composed in genres other than jazz and popular.

The instrument is played sitting down with a slightly more comfortable playing position than the violin and viola, and the player can look and see what they are attempting to do, which makes things a little easier. In common with the violin and viola, the left hand 'stops' the strings against the fingerboard while the right hand draws the bow over the strings. Cello strings are tuned to C–G–D–A, and music for it is written mostly in the bass clef with occasional use of the tenor clef. Beginners need not worry about the tenor clef as its use will not arise in the earlier stages of learning.

In terms of learning the 'cello, the same principles apply as with the violin and viola. Although not an easy instrument to play, the 'cello may produce more pleasing results, more quickly than the violin, for many learners. Adults often find the 'cello an easier instrument to start on than the violin or viola. One factor in this is the size of the instrument, which makes it a little easier for larger adult hands, coupled with the way the instrument is played, which allows the player to see what they are doing more easily. Even a player with modest facility on the instrument will be welcome in an amateur ensemble as there is nearly always a shortage of instruments to play the lower, bass notes of a piece. This will also apply as more progress is made and playing opportunities are sought in local amateur orchestras and ensembles. The difficulties associated with playing the violin, using each hand independently, apply equally to the 'cello.

Beginners' instruments are more modestly priced, but as with the violin, the sky is the limit for a really good one. The purchase price is reasonable for a mid-range instrument, and there is fairly ready availability on the secondhand market. As with all instruments, follow your teacher's advice when buying a new or secondhand instrument. Running costs are minimal, with replacement strings and occasional maintenance being the main items. However, 'cellos are easily damaged, particularly in the hurly burly of life, and repairs can be very costly.

Like violins, 'cellos are available in scaled-down sizes for the smaller beginner. Cases range from the canvas cover (now almost historic), which affords minimal protection, to lightweight hard cases which will survive almost anything. Secondhand instruments may be sold without a case, so beware of this additional cost which you may incur. A case is essential for taking the instrument to lessons or rehearsals.

Double Bass

The double bass is the largest and lowest-pitched member of the string family, with four strings tuned to E–A–D–G. Symphony orchestras may have as many as eight double basses, chamber orchestras perhaps just two, and smaller ensembles usually have one. The repertoire for double bass embraces the full range of orchestral and string music, and it is also found in the symphonic wind band and, of course, in jazz ensembles. It is a versatile instrument, and players can transfer easily to electric bass for access to contemporary popular music.

The player stands, or sits on a high stool, and the instrument rests on a spike. The left hand 'stops' the strings against the fingerboard, while the right hand draws the bow over the strings. In jazz ensembles, the bass is usually played pizzicato, the strings plucked by the right hand.

The double bass attracts comparatively few learners, despite being in many respects easier than the violin, viola or 'cello, so in that sense, it is a great instrument to choose, as double bass players are welcomed in many different ensembles. Its size means it is musically forgiving, and although not easier to play to a very high standard, pitch inaccuracies and sound imperfections will be much less noticeable. The transition to bass guitar will be easy for most players interested in moving to jazz or popular music, as they will find the instrument less physically demanding than its counterpart.

The double bass is more expensive than the violin, viola or 'cello.

The purchase price is significant, and although the secondhand market is quite good and there are a large number of instruments in circulation, finding a good one can be difficult. Running costs are minimal, although replacing the strings, which fortunately does not happen too often, can be costly.

The double bass is quite heavy and cumbersome, and is not easily transported. It is made in differing sizes, and many adult players use a three-quarter size instrument. Of all the orchestral stringed instruments, the double bass is in many respects the most attractive to go for. Music arranged for it in transcriptions for amateur orchestras is often less demanding than the parts played by the violins, violas and cellos, and the shortage of players means there are likely to be more opportunities to take part in ensembles. Since the 1980s it has been made in a format known as the mini-bass, to encourage younger and smaller learners to take it up.

PLUCKED STRINGED INSTRUMENTS

Plucked strings include the harp, guitar, electric guitar, electric bass, mandolin, ukelele, balalaika and banjo.

Harp

The harp exists in two main formats: the lever harp and the pedal harp. In both forms of the instrument you change the tuning of the strings by using either a lever, or pedals. The lever harp is also known as the clarsach, folk, traditional, non-pedal, small, Scottish, Irish or Celtic harp. Orchestral music, or chromatic music, will be written almost certainly for the pedal harp, which dates from the early nineteenth century, as its mechanism allows the player to change the pitch of the strings by using foot pedals whilst continuing to play. The lever harp is more suited

Concert harp.

to traditional or folk-based music, which is generally less chromatic and often based on modes. Lever harps are made in a variety of sizes, but are significantly smaller and cheaper to purchase than pedal harps. The pedal harp is large, heavy, mechanically complex and expensive whether secondhand or new. Its range is similar to that of a piano, and it uses a system of pedals to change the notes produced by plucking the forty-six strings, which are fewer in number than those of a piano. There is more information about the smaller harps used in traditional music further on in this chapter. The pedal harp came to prominence in the orchestrations of Romantic and twentieth-century composers. Its ability to add colour and mood to a piece made it an essential for the composer's palette.

To play either sort of harp, you sit with the instrument in front of you, plucking the strings using both hands, one on each side of the instrument. All your fingers are used except the little ones.

Harp teachers are quite scarce, and in many respects, learning to play the harp may be a bigger commitment for learners than many other instruments, so special consideration and plenty of time should be given to the decision-making process. Many teachers will allow or encourage an adult beginner to start lessons without owning an instrument, and allow six or more months to help a learner to decide whether they really want to go further with it and commit to purchasing. In common with an instrument such as the piano, the harp presents the player with all the notes they will need, and in one sense it is simply a question of plucking the right string at the right moment to get the note you require.

Orchestral pedal harps are expensive, and there is only a limited and rather knowledgeable secondhand market. Maintenance is also costly. In fact the harp will probably cost as much as the car you will need to transport it! Additional expenditure in the form of a cover, a trolley for moving it, mechanical repairs and replacement strings make the orchestral harp an instrument to be considered very carefully if it's your final choice. Harps are getting on for 2m (7ft) in length and weigh about 35kg (80lb).

Acoustic and Electric Guitars

Acoustic and electric guitars have six strings tuned to E–A–D–G–B–E. There is also a twelve-string version which grew in popularity from the 1920s onwards, in blues and folk music especially. The lower four strings on this guitar are tuned an octave apart, and it produces a richer, more shimmering sound. The fingerboard on most guitars has frets (metal strips across it), to help the player see and feel where the fingers go. A basic acoustic guitar is an inexpensive and relatively fragile instrument, usually supplied with a soft cover. It is a quiet, gentle instrument, which, when strummed, can play chords as an accompaniment to a sung melody, or melodies themselves when picked with the fingers or a plectrum, including the classical compositions of a wide range of composers.

The rise of the electric guitar from the 1950s has seen the instrument most commonly played in pop groups, where the player usually relies on memorizing the music, but as with the bass guitar, drums and keyboards, those who learn to read from notation or chord symbols gain quicker access to a much broader repertoire.

The acoustic instrument is either held by a neck strap, for styles other than classical music, with the strings plucked or strummed by the right hand. The player may use a plectrum with which to strum or pick the notes. The classical guitar is rested on the player's lap without use of a strap, but needs a small footstool. Electric guitars always use straps and plectrums.

In schools, guitars are often taught in large groups, up to, and sometimes beyond, whole class size. Different versions of the basic model are available, each designed to play different styles of music. Your teacher will be able to advise you on the best sort for your beginner needs. The term 'classical' guitar describes the sort of guitar designed for playing the classical music written for it.

The guitar is a popular and versatile instrument, and one of the few easily portable musical instruments that can provide a chordal accompaniment for a singer. Guitars are easy to carry. Playing involves high levels of co-ordination, and music written for classical guitar can look, and be, difficult to read, especially for those unfamiliar with its notation. Some players learn to read from standard notation, others from tablature referred to as 'tab', and others from chords. Tablature is a more pictorial form of notation related directly to the strings on the instrument and the placing of the fingers.

There is a ready secondhand market for electric and acoustic guitars. Many learners will prefer to buy a new acoustic guitar, as prices are quite modest for a beginner's instrument. Buying a secondhand electric guitar means checking that both music and electrics are up to scratch.

The electric guitar is more expensive than the acoustic guitar, given that it will usually be necessary to buy an amplifier as well – and of course is capable of making more noise when being practised, although headphones are always an option!

Electric Bass Guitar

The bass guitar is tuned to the same notes as the string double bass, E-A-D-G, and is essentially an electronic version of that instrument. It is electronically amplified like the electric guitar, and is easier to carry than a double bass, although it does require an amplifier which may add to the initial expense and subsequent difficulties with transportation. The instrument was developed in the 1920s, and mass production began in the 1950s.

The bass guitar can provide a bass part in any form of jazz or popular music ensemble, combo or band. Bass players are sought after, particularly those who can work from notation in addition to playing by ear. It is played in all kinds of popular music and jazz ensembles, and is easier to learn than the six-string guitar, although it has slightly fewer capabilities. Music for electric bass guitar is written in the bass clef. Pop music is usually played from memory, and consequently some bass players do not learn to read music. Some learn to interpret chord symbols or tablature, rather than traditional Western notation. Those who do learn to read music gain immediate access to more playing opportunities across a broader variety of styles, and learning to read from notation is almost certainly worth the effort for adult beginners.

The bass guitar requires co-ordination of both hands, but is a little easier to play than a six-string guitar. It is rarely, if ever, played as a solo instrument, and relies on ensemble music-making. It is a single note instrument, although it can play chords. In many respects it is an ideal beginners' instrument if it suits the sort of music you would like to play, and progress can be quite rapid.

There are many secondhand instruments available, but both the musical qualities and electrical reliability of the instrument need to be tested before purchase. New instruments are modestly priced, although you may need expert help to check the quality and accuracy of the fingerboard and frets.

Lute, Mandolin, Ukulele, Banjo, Balalaika

Private teachers specializing in these instruments may be quite scarce, and many teacher-players may play one of them as a second or third instrument. The fact that all of them, with the exception of the ukelele, are less commonly taught may give them an added appeal for some learners.

Lute

The lute's name and shape are derived from the Arabic 'ud' or 'oud', an instrument which came to Europe in the Middle Ages. Its popu-

Lute, mandolin, ukulele, banjo and guitar. NAHARIYANI

larity from the late fifteenth century and for the following 150 years is perhaps similar to the guitar's popularity today. The instrument is found in numerous different forms, but the basic shape is similar to a bowl-backed mandolin, but much larger. The lute usually has between fifteen and twenty-four strings; these are mostly grouped in twos, and are referred to as courses. A person who plays the lute is referred to as a 'lutenist'. The strings are plucked, and it is quite a difficult instrument to tune. The Indian sitar was developed in northern India at the same time as the lute.

Lutes are quite expensive to purchase and quite vulnerable. By the end of the seventeenth century the lute's days as a popular instrument were numbered, not least because its dynamic range is small and it could not compete when played in ensembles with other instruments, and especially in the developing orchestra.

Mandolin
The mandolin belongs to the lute family, and is found in two

versions: the Neapolitan or bowl-backed mandolin, and the flat-backed mandolin. Both versions have eight strings and they are tuned in pairs: G-G – D-D – A-A – E-E, and both versions are played with a plectrum. It is predominantly a melody instrument. It is the Neapolitan version that is referred to in *Captain Corelli's Mandolin*, the novel by Louis de Bernières, which may have drawn it to your attention.

Ukulele

The ukulele is a cross between a mandolin and a guitar. It originated in the nineteenth century as a Hawaiian adaptation of a Portuguese instrument, which had been introduced to Hawaii by Portuguese immigrants. It gained popularity in the United States during the early twentieth century, and from there spread internationally. In its soprano form it is small and highly portable, with four strings tuned to A–E–C–G. The ukulele looks like a miniature guitar, and was made famous by the musical hall artiste, George Formby, in the performances of his own songs.

There are three larger instruments in the ukulele family, with up to eight strings. In recent years the ukulele has enjoyed a huge resurgence in popularity, since it was taken up by many Music Services as the instrument of choice for whole class instrumental tuition.

Banjo

The banjo is a long-necked, four-, five- or six-stringed instrument, the five-string being the most common; the most usual tuning for it is G–D–B–G–D, although there are numerous alternatives. It was taken to North America by slaves from Africa, and then to Europe where it became part of the music-hall tradition. It is similar in size to the mandolin, but with a longer neck. The body of the instrument is covered with skin, or on contemporary instruments a plastic membrane, which increases its resonance.

The Balalaika

The balalaika is used not only for folk music but also in bands and orchestras in Russia. It has a triangular body and long neck, with three strings often tuned to E-E-A. It comes in a variety of sizes constituting a complete family of instruments.

General Observations on these Instruments

Mandolins are modestly priced and quite robust instruments. Ukuleles (soprano) can be purchased cheaply and are easy to look after. They are available as traditional wooden instruments, or made from polycarbonate materials. Banjos are modestly priced and easy to look after. Balalaikas are more expensive, with lutes being the most expensive. Whilst anyone learning any of these instruments will benefit from a good teacher, the ukulele and banjo in particular may just as easily be self-taught. If you to choose to learn to play the lute you really will benefit from the input of a teacher. All these instruments are relatively light to carry, with the soprano ukulele being the smallest, lightest and most portable of all, and it is now available in a range of styles, colours and materials to suit most pockets.

Before beginning to learn any of these instruments it may be as well to find out what ensemble opportunities exist in your locality, as it could be frustrating to get off to a flying start but then be thwarted because you are unable to make music with any suitable groups nearby.

BRASS INSTRUMENTS

Tenor horn, sousaphone, french horn, trombone, trumpet and bugle.
NAHARIYANI

Brass instruments include the cornet, trumpet, pocket trumpet, flugelhorn, French horn, trombone, tenor horn, baritone horn, euphonium, tuba and sousaphone.

Although there are many brass instruments in this extended family, only the ones listed above are commonly taught to beginners today. In reality, many beginners will start on a cornet, trumpet, tenor or baritone horn, or a trombone, and will perhaps be guided towards a lower-pitched instrument by their teacher. All the instruments on the list belong to this family because the sound is made by blowing through a detachable metal mouthpiece into a metal tube. The player uses three or four valves, or on the trombone a slide, to alter the length of the metal tube, and this, combined with different lip tensions and air pressure, enables notes of different pitch to be produced.

Brass instruments are played in brass or silver bands, military bands, orchestras, big bands, jazz bands, marching bands and many other ensembles. The distinction between brass and silver bands comes from the days when 'brass' instruments tended to be cheaper than 'silver' ones. Now, however, the costs are similar, and the distinction between brass and silver bands is generally not made. There is also a substantial quantity of music written for individual brass instruments and piano.

Orchestral brass players may be separate from brass-band players, but in the earliest stages of learning such divisions will be less important. Some instruments, such as the tenor horn, baritone and euphonium, are used mainly in bands rather than as orchestral instruments, but it is likely there will be opportunities in music centres for school-age learners for all the brass family.

Brass bands have a musical culture and life of their own. There are many very high quality brass bands, and most of them run junior and training bands, which enable children and adults to join as complete beginners and learn from scratch as part of an ensemble. Brass bands also play in competitions against one another, and have their own leagues and so on. Competition playing undoubtedly helps to drive up standards, although some musicians, mainly outside the brass-band world, express a dislike for the notion of competition in musical performances of the same piece. Music written for brass bands is always written in the treble clef, no matter how low-pitched the instrument, but whether you choose to learn a trumpet to play in a brass band or in an orchestra, this need not concern you at the outset.

Brass players tend to stick together. They tend to have a 'can do' attitude to playing, which perhaps stems from the fact that they know their sheer volume can musically obliterate any other orchestral or band section if they choose to! The brass player can take her instrument out of the case and start playing while the woodwind player is putting her instrument together and searching for a reed, and the string player is trying to tune her instrument. Brass players, particularly on trumpets and horns, learn to deal with transposition as part of the process of learning.

Brass instruments do require energy and stamina, but for most learners this does not pose a problem. Well played brass instruments provide the power to cut through an orchestral or big band texture, and can easily dominate an orchestra or band's sound. They provide fanfare, pomp and majesty, or melancholy, as in 'The Last Post', played on Remembrance Day.

Cornet and Trumpet

The cornet and trumpet are the smallest and most popular instruments of the brass family. The cornet, on which sounds are produced in a similar way to the trumpet, has the same range of notes, and both have three valves. The pocket trumpet is a miniaturized version of the standard B flat (Bb) trumpet and really something of a novelty item, perhaps suitable for a professional player to use for practice when travelling, and perhaps not quite so suitable for beginners, but it can be useful for practice sessions by experienced players. The flugelhorn has a more conical bore than the trumpet and plays lower-pitched notes more readily. Again, it is not really a beginners' instrument, and is often used in jazz ensembles. Transferring from the trumpet to the flugelhorn is relatively easy.

Music written for the trumpet is found from the Baroque period onwards, and the instrument features in the orchestral music of Haydn, Mozart and Beethoven, through the Romantic era to the twentieth century and on to the present day. The trumpet is also found in wind bands, marching bands, military bands and jazz ensembles of all kinds. The cornet is more strongly associated with the brass band and military band.

Different pitches are produced by a combination of pressing the valves and using the lips to vibrate the air that is blown through the mouthpiece in different ways. It is the harmonic series that provides the basic notes of the instrument, and the operation of the valves that access other bits of tubing of differing lengths, which provide the notes in between the harmonics. Gaining mastery of this combination of harmonics and valved notes is the essence of brass playing, and once you develop some initial fluency on the trumpet, it is possible to move fairly easily to one of the lower-pitched brass instruments. Teachers may recommend this to those who find playing the higher-pitched notes on the trumpet difficult.

Brass bands use cornets rather than trumpets, and many learners find that they really like the simplicity of the cornet and the trumpet. This may be as much to do with the fact that there are just three valves to press down, in their various combinations, as with the fact that the player is producing a series of notes which are the natural harmonics produced by any vibrating object.

Success with playing the trumpet, cornet or any brass instrument, is dependent on regular practice to 'keep your lip in'. There are no shortcuts with this, and it is definitely not an instrument that can only be practised the day before your lesson or a rehearsal, if you want to make real progress. When you play a note on the trumpet, everyone in the ensemble knows about it, so adults who learn the instrument need a degree of self-confidence with which to start. Although the first few months of learning to play the trumpet or cornet can be aurally quite challenging, most beginners acquire enough control of sound production to enable them to play simple melodies within, say, a couple of months' regular weekly lessons.

Running costs include occasional maintenance, a mouthpiece, and valve oil. The purchase price of either a new trumpet or cornet is relatively modest, and although the secondhand market is good, many learners may prefer to buy a new one. The detachable mouthpiece should be cleaned regularly. Both cornet and trumpet can be damaged quite easily, and although most dents can be fairly readily removed, the resulting trips to the repairers can be costly over time!

Both instruments weigh around less than a couple of kilos (about 2kg/4lb), and modern cases are both durable and light.

French Horn

The French horn is derived from the hunting horn, and took its place in the classical orchestra of Mozart and Haydn in the eighteenth century. It is used in military bands, windbands and, of course, the symphony orchestra, but is only found rarely in jazz ensembles. It is not used in brass bands where it is replaced by the tenor and baritone horns. In the orchestrations of the great Romantic composers such as Brahms and Mahler, Wagner and Strauss, it comes into its own and was adopted similarly by many film composers in the late twentieth century. Have a listen to the scores of any of the James Bond films, and you will hear plenty of horn playing.

Composers use the French horn both as a solo instrument – for example, the opening of the second movement of Tchaikovsky's fifth symphony – and because they can make a sound which makes strings and woodwind mix together very well, adding something to the texture that creates an almost completely new sound from the blend of instruments.

The sound is produced in a similar way to that of other brass instruments, but the main difference is that the player puts his hand in the bell of the instrument both to support it and to change the pitch of some notes. This is called hand-stopping. The French horn is quite a difficult instrument to play, and generally requires more perseverance, and even French horn players say this. It is essential to be able to hear the sound you want to make before attempting to play it, and good teachers will check your aural perception before encouraging you to embark on a series of lessons. It is probably easier to play a wrong note on the French horn by mis-pitching it, than on any other brass instrument. That said, French horn players are always welcome in amateur orchestras where there may be a shortage of good players.

French horns are more expensive to buy than trumpets or trombones, perhaps because they are more complicated to make, and perhaps because relatively few are sold, compared with the trumpet, for example. The detachable mouthpiece should be cleaned regularly. French horns can be quite heavy to carry, and the shape of most cases, which follow the contours of the instrument, means that they are more cumbersome than some other brass family instruments.

Trombone

The name 'trombone' literally means 'large trumpet'. It is the only member of the brass family which usually has a slide, rather than valves, although a valved version is available – jazz musician Bob Brookmeyer always used this form of the instrument. The trombone dates back to the Renaissance, and until the early eighteenth century was known as a sackbut.

The modern instrument that is most commonly played is the tenor trombone pitched in B flat (Bb). Although described as a B flat instrument it is, confusingly and unlike the B flat (Bb) trumpet, not a transposing instrument. The modern orchestral trombonist reads music written for it in the bass clef, but their counterpart in the brass band reads music written in the treble clef, which is written as for a transposing instrument. If you are thinking about learning the trombone you need have no concern about the slightly complicated sounding issue of transposition, as your teacher will be able to explain it to you and it is highly unlikely to pose you any sort of difficulty. There is also a bass trombone, but as a beginner you would expect to start on the tenor version of the instrument.

Mozart wrote some interesting parts for the trombone – for example, the 'tuba mirum' in his *Requiem*. Today it features in music written for windband, orchestra and in jazz ensembles. Its ability to slide (glissando) between notes means that it can produce comic effects, as in, for example, *The Acrobat*, by composer John Greenwood, as well as more threatening sounds. The trombone's repertoire ranges from the majestic to the comic, so most players will be able to find a musical style that suits them.

The player changes the pitch of the note by a combination of moving the slide to the position of one of the notes in the harmonic series, and adjusting his/her embouchure. Although a slightly more difficult instrument to handle than the trumpet, it is an easier one on which to make a sound, and in most terms a slightly easier instrument for the beginner brass player. As ever, a good teacher will help you to find the right brass instrument to suit your natural embouchure.

The trombone is a modestly priced instrument, and although there is a good secondhand market, most learners will probably prefer to buy a new one. In recent years the pbone, a plastic trombone, has come on to the market, providing a very practical and cheaper alternative instrument for beginner trombonists; it is available in a variety of colours. The detachable mouthpiece should be cleaned regularly, and the slide must be looked after very carefully. The slide of a metal trombone is easily dented or knocked out of true, and without a free-moving slide it is impossible to play the instrument well. The trombone is quite large to carry around, and consideration may need to be given to this.

Tenor Horn

The tenor horn was invented in the middle of the nineteenth century as the alto voice in the saxhorn family, which along with the saxophone family was developed by the Belgian musical instrument designer and musician who played the flute and clarinet, Adolphe Sax. In the UK, the name 'alto' was dropped in favour of 'tenor'. The tenor horn should not be confused with the French horn.

There is a strong network of brass bands across the UK, most of which, if not all, welcome beginners. Brass bands play music from a broad range of musical styles, and focus on providing many performance opportunities. The tenor horn does not figure in orchestral writing, so a beginner may be less welcome in a local amateur orchestra if that ensemble has the full complement of players. As a tenor horn player, however, you are likely to be welcomed in a windband or concert band.

It is generally easier to pitch notes on the tenor horn than on the trumpet and cornet, and the instrument uses a slightly more relaxed embouchure. Adult beginners and children find this one of the easier brass instruments on which to start. Playing a brass-band instrument means that you could be part of an ensemble which, both in the way that it rehearses, as in the way it looks after its members, will make you feel part of its family group. Many brass bands offer tuition, often free, that simply involves a beginner 'sitting in', and being helped by older, more experienced players. For would-be brass players – cornet players, tenor and baritone horns and trombonists – this can be an ideal way of finding out if you like these instruments and this form of music-making.

New instruments are not too expensive, and there is a steady secondhand market. The detachable mouthpiece should be cleaned regularly. The tenor horn is neither too heavy to hold, nor to carry, and is easy to look after.

Baritone Horn

The baritone horn is pitched in B flat (Bb), and is usually found only in brass bands and windbands, as distinct from orchestras. Like the tenor horn it 'speaks', or makes a sound, more easily than the French horn and is neither too heavy nor too large to carry around. Like the tenor horn, it belongs to the saxhorn family, and its relations in the brass world are the trumpet and trombone, as all three have a cylindrical bore. It is smaller and more compact than the euphonium. In the UK, brass-band music for baritone horn is written in the treble clef.

The baritone horn's real repertoire is that of the brass band, although it is welcomed in many windbands. It is easier to pitch than the trumpet and cornet, and uses a slightly more relaxed embouchure. Like the trumpet, cornet, tenor horn and euphonium, it has three valves.

The baritone horn, like the tenor horn, is generally one of the easier brass instruments on which to start, and the advantages of learning a brass instrument lie in the community spirit, referred to earlier in the section on tenor horn. It is easy to look after, and new instruments are not too expensive. The detachable mouthpiece should be cleaned regularly. There is a steady secondhand market.

Euphonium

The euphonium looks like a large baritone horn, and there are many similarities between the two instruments. They are both pitched in B flat (Bb). Orchestral euphonium parts are written in the bass clef, and brass-band parts are written in the treble clef, but the sounds produced are the same, regardless of which notation is used.

The euphonium has a wider bore than other brass instruments, almost conical. It is a wind- and brass-band instrument rather than an orchestral one. In the UK, brass-band music for euphonium is written in the treble clef. To play it, you hold the instrument with one hand and press the valves with the other.

Few beginners are likely to start on this instrument; most will be guided by their teacher, having started on a higher-pitched brass instrument. Here, your teacher's recommendation is of vital importance, and he or she may be able to recognize that you have potential, and that the cornet or tenor horn is not the right instrument for you; you will certainly benefit from being guided in this situation.

Euphoniums are quite expensive. As with all brass instruments, maintenance should not be too costly, although dents are easily acquired. The detachable mouthpiece should be cleaned regularly. Brass instruments are not necessarily as robust as they may look.

The euphonium is big and quite heavy without its case. It is less easy to carry around than many instruments, and there is certainly no question of pretending you don't play it. The sound is quite gentle, so practising at home should not upset the rest of the family, or your neighbours, too much.

Tuba

The tuba is similar in appearance to the euphonium, but it is bigger and its origins are in fact different. Although a large and somewhat unwieldy instrument, the tuba is always very much in demand because it plays the bass part in ensembles. There is usually one in an orchestra, providing the bass notes for the brass section and/or strengthening the woodwind or string bass parts.

There may be several tubas in a brass band, where they are known as E flat (Eb), B flat (Bb), or double E flat (EEb) and double B flat (BBb) basses. Double simply refers to a larger, lower-pitched version of the instrument, and the E flat (Eb) and B flat (Bb) refers to the two pitches in which it is made. A good teacher will explain all this to you, and it need not concern you as a beginner. To play the instrument you rest it on your knee, holding it with one hand, while pressing the valves with the other.

The embouchure is easier to master than, say, the trumpet, and the tuba may be chosen after starting on a different higher-pitched brass instrument. It may not be a first choice for beginners, and as with the French, tenor and baritone horns, it is an instrument that learners are often encouraged to transfer to by their teacher. As with other bass instruments, such as the bassoon or string double bass, the ensemble part which they play may be a little less demanding than those played by higher-pitched instruments, but there is a true sense of leadership for players who provide the bass to an ensemble. The euphonium is a more expensive instrument than a trumpet, French horn or trombone.

It is a large and heavy instrument to carry without its case. Secondhand instruments are available, but check that they have not been repaired inexpertly, which could result in a loss of tone on certain notes. Advice and guidance from your teacher is essential. New instruments are expensive.

Sousaphone

The sousaphone is an American marching band instrument, and was developed at the end of the nineteenth century for the composer of many well known marches, John Philip Sousa. He wanted a tuba that it was possible to march with, and which would project its sound over the band. The instrument used at the time was the helicon, and Sousa wanted to improve on this instrument. In other respects the sousaphone is similar to the tuba. The sousaphone also became popular in the traditional jazz bands of the 1920s.

WOODWIND

Woodwind includes ocarina, tinwhistle penny whistle or whistle, piccolo, recorder, flute, fife, oboe, cor anglais, oboe d'amore, clarinet, bassoon and saxophone.

Flute. PIXABAY

Clarinet.
PAVEL SAZONOV

Woodwind instruments derive their name from the simple fact that in the past they were all made of wood, and they make their sound by having wind blown through them. However, saxophones, which are made of metal, were added to the family in the mid-nineteenth century, and since the beginning of the last century, most flutes and piccolos have been made of metal. Clarinets and saxophones use what are described as single reeds, oboes and bassoons use double reeds, and ocarinas, recorders, fifes, flutes and piccolos do not have a reed. The recorder, flute, oboe, B flat (Bb) clarinet, bassoon and saxophone are the most commonly taught woodwind instruments.

Bassoon. PIXABAY

The classical orchestra, from the time of Mozart and Haydn, has two each of flutes, oboes, clarinets and bassoons comprising its woodwind section. In the nineteenth century the orchestra expanded and often included double the number of woodwind instruments, or additional members of the woodwind family according to the composer's preference. The military band and symphonic wind-band have extended the range of woodwind instruments within

Oboe. PIXABAY

Saxophone. PRESSMASTER

their ranks, but only the saxophone, B flat (Bb) clarinet and flute are commonly found in jazz ensembles.

Many woodwind players double, or play on more than one instrument of the woodwind family, but it is usual to concentrate on one instrument at the outset of learning until some degree of confidence is achieved, before moving to a second or subsequent instruments. The production of sound on the clarinets and saxophones is similar, as is the production of sound on the two double-reed instruments. Woodwind players have instruments that on the one hand are quite robust, when compared for example with stringed instruments, but each one is reliant on complex keywork mechanisms to make them play, and oboes, bassoons and clarinets that are made of wood, are sensitive to temperature and moisture. Reeds are a permanent source of mild concern for most professional players, who are forever seeking the perfect reed that will allow them to access low and high notes, loud and quiet passages with equal ease. The music written for woodwind instruments in an orchestra is a mixture of technically demanding passages and much simpler ones.

In recent years, smaller versions of most of the woodwind family of instruments have been developed to enable young beginners, primary school-aged children, to start learning them, and these are considered at the end of this section.

Ocarina

The ocarina is really a traditional or folk-music instrument, which dates back many thousands of years. It is found in various forms across a range of cultures. Perhaps its greatest advantage over the recorder is that if you blow it very hard it just doesn't make a sound, whereas a recorder will emit a very shrill, piercing note. In addition to the folk music from whence it originated, there is a wide range of fairly recently published arrangements of all sorts of music for the ocarina. It has the same basic range of notes as the recorder, and blends well with that instrument.

The modern-day version, often made of plastic, is potato shaped, fits neatly into a small cupped hand, can be worn on a lanyard around the neck, and makes its sound in the same way as the recorder. It is an easy instrument on which to make a sound, and simple tunes can be learned very quickly.

For many classroom teachers it provides a slightly gentler sounding alternative to the recorder, and it is available in different sizes, so giving a larger range of notes, thus making ensemble music more accessible and pleasant sounding. The ocarina is an ideal starter instrument for young children if there is an enthusiastic ocarina group teacher available, and there is no reason why an adult shouldn't try one. By starting with an instrument such as the ocarina, you can explore issues associated with music-making and make a more informed decision about which instrument you may want to move on to next. It plays a role in traditional music, and you may be attracted to it, as an adult learner, for that reason.

The ocarina is one of the cheapest musical instruments available, with no real running costs other than perhaps an occasional replacement for the optional lanyard. Ocarinas come in a range of sizes, the smallest being no bigger than a matchbox and weighing a few grams.

Tin Whistle, Penny Whistle or Whistle

The whistle is a simple, six-holed instrument that belongs with the woodwind family, although it is commonly made of metal. It dates back to music of pre-historic times, and has strong roots in traditional music. When the process of tin plating developed in the late eighteenth century it could be manufactured cheaply, and thus became cheaply and readily available, and its popularity spread. In many respects its place in education has been taken by the recorder, which was popularized in the UK through the work of recorder player Dr Carl Dolmetsch, who invented the plastic version of the instrument.

Descant Recorder

The recorder is a serious musical instrument as well as being fun to play. In the fifteenth century recorder consorts, or groups, consisted of sopranino, descant, treble, tenor and bass recorders, which played music specially written for them. Musically close to the recorder is the ocarina, which is again an easy instrument on which to make a sound. Most schools have recorders, and many adults will remember an early encounter with a recorder on their musical journey. If this wasn't such a good experience for you, don't write off the instrument just for that reason.

There is a huge repertoire for the recorder, extending from music composed for it as a consort instrument, through to arrangements of contemporary pop music and film scores. The player places the mouthpiece between his lips, and blows gently into and through the instrument. The stream of air is directed through a windway to a point where it is split, which sets it vibrating in such a way as to produce a musical sound.

The recorder is always a favourite in schools and with children, because, like the ocarina, it is easy to make a sound – for the same reason it is sometimes less popular with parents. Although it is often used as a whole-class instrument in schools, many teachers form recorder groups, introducing the other instruments from the recorder family. There is plenty of contemporary music written for such groups, as well as numerous arrangements of currently popular music. Like all instruments, it is difficult to play really well.

The purchase price is modest, and consequently the secondhand market is almost non-existent as learners will almost certainly want a new instrument. Although recorders can be purchased very cheaply it is worth paying a little more than the minimum in order to have an instrument with a better tone and accuracy of tuning in manufacture. Running costs are minimal. The instrument can fit inside a coat pocket, and weighs no more than a few grams.

Recorders are traditionally made of wood, but instruments for beginners are often made of plastic and can make a perfectly good sound. There is no minimum or maximum age limit here, and ease of tone production is coupled with the benefit of a very modest price.

Flute (Piccolo)

Flutes were originally made of wood, but today, most are made of metal. The piccolo, a smaller and higher-pitched version of the flute, used by composers of orchestral music to provide particularly high notes, is not generally thought of as a suitable instrument for beginners. The flute family also includes alto and bass instruments, to which players may extend their expertise having gained a degree of mastery of the flute. These lower-pitched instruments are used principally in flute choirs, or for particular effects in orchestral or band scoring.

The flute plays in orchestras, windbands, wind quintets and jazz ensembles, and there is a huge repertoire for the instrument, covering many styles of music. It can be played as a solo instrument or accompanied by the piano. The flute is a very popular instrument, which could mean that within your local community there is competition for places in a band or orchestra. This is unlikely to be a serious consideration when starting the instrument, but may need to be kept in mind. It also provides the probable advantage for a beginner of being able to sit next to someone with more experience when you join an ensemble.

The player holds the instrument to one side and blows air across the mouthpiece, a hole near one end of the instrument. Occasionally learners find that making a sound is initially difficult, and to an extent it depends on the individual's physical make-up, namely the shape of the mouth and jaw, combined with the position of the teeth. Few learners find it impossible to make a sound, and an experienced teacher should be able to get almost anyone to make a note. Such a teacher can usually tell just by looking at a potential student whether or not they are likely to find playing the flute easy or more difficult.

Once a sound has been established, the player must get used to holding the flute to one side of their head. Most models of flute use plateau keywork, where the player's fingers press keys which in turn cover the holes. This, in turn, means that the player's fingers don't have to be particularly big, nor stretch too far.

The purchase price of a flute is relatively modest, and the second-hand market is good. Running costs include occasional maintenance, and in common with the other woodwind family instruments, beginners should not attempt to tighten or loosen the many small screws that are visible. Some of these screws hold keywork in place and others are adjusters. To make adjustment needs expertise, so it is best left to a professional repairer, or your teacher, who will often be able to carry out such work.

Flutes are light and easy to carry, and their cases are unobtrusive. They are now available with a curved head joint, which means that the total length is reduced. This means that smaller adults, or younger children, will be able to reach out far enough to hold it, which they may not be able to do with the normal flute.

Oboe, Cor Anglais, Oboe d'Amore

The oboe developed in Baroque times and is best suited to orchestral and ensemble work, including the wind quintet. It also has a place in modern windbands and military bands. Other instruments that belong to the oboe family are the cor anglais and the oboe d'amore. The cor anglais is an orchestral instrument that is often taken up by oboists, but only after they become proficient on the oboe. It is not a beginners' instrument. The oboe d'amore is similarly not a beginners' instrument, and features chiefly in orchestral music of the eighteenth century.

The oboe is at its best playing music originally written for it, rather than transcriptions of other works. Its core repertoire is the music of the Baroque era and the orchestra of the Classical and Romantic eras. It is found less frequently in jazz or popular music.

Beginner oboists need encouragement and a good degree of self-belief. The sound is made by placing the double reed between the lips and blowing air through the narrow gap between the two reeds and into the instrument. When the instrument is played well, its haunting quality and pastoral sounds make it very special. The instrument may appeal to you as a learner if you are more interested in 'serious' music, or if you care to enjoy playing one sort of music on the oboe, and other styles on another instrument, or through singing.

It is perhaps the hardest woodwind instrument for beginners to master because of its double reed, which is easily damaged, and highly sensitive in terms of making the sound. At the beginning, the oboe can easily tend to produce a coarse and rather harsh, penetrating sound, reminding us of its origins as an instrument to be played out of doors. Oboists can play arrangements of lighter music in windbands and concert bands, but will find it more difficult to join jazz groups. Developing control and mastery of the sound and tone is difficult. Reeds will need to be purchased regularly, and finding a good reed is, for the beginner, largely a matter of luck. Good oboe players are scarce and therefore highly sought after.

The purchase price for an oboe is relatively modest, although a little more expensive than either the flute or the clarinet. There are comparatively few good instruments on the secondhand market. Running costs include reeds, and occasional maintenance, which should be carried out by an experienced technician. Experienced players may make or prepare their own reeds, but this is an exacting task and not for the beginner player. The instrument is small and not heavy to carry. It fits in a small, compact case.

Clarinet

Clarinets were originally made of African hardwood, boxwood or grenadilla, and when made of these natural materials they are very sensitive to the impact of the warm moist air from the player blowing through the instrument. If the wood was not properly seasoned or subsequently looked after, the instrument could easily split. Modern, high quality instruments are made of wood, but there is also a range of instruments made of artificial materials, and these are ideal for beginners and can also be played to a high standard as well. These instruments are designed for low maintenance and a long playing life.

The clarinet family includes alto, bass, contra-alto and contra-bass. The sound is made in a similar way with all of them. Orchestral players use a B flat (Bb) clarinet and an A clarinet. Both instruments are essentially the same in appearance and in the way you play them, with the A clarinet pitched one semitone lower than the B flat. Beginners need only have one instrument, the B flat (Bb), which will suffice for several years of learning.

The clarinet developed in the eighteenth century and was a favourite of Mozart, who wrote a concerto for it. It is a member of the symphony orchestra, and is of equal value in jazz ensembles, windbands and chamber music, and thus often described as a versatile instrument.

The regular B flat (Bb) instrument is usually assembled each time it is played, and the reed attached to the mouthpiece. The mouthpiece goes into the player's mouth with the reed resting on the lower lip, which is placed over the bottom teeth. By closing your mouth around the reed and mouthpiece and blowing air between them, the column of air inside the instrument is set in vibration, which produces the sound. The reed is quite fragile and easily damaged. The slightest amount of damage affects the reed's ability to vibrate and thus the sound quality, or even the potential to enable the player to produce a sound at all. Plastic reeds are available but are generally regarded as a poor substitute for the real thing by more experienced players, because they are less sensitive.

The clarinet is a popular choice for beginners. In simple terms it plays the right note if your fingers are in the right place, although it is very possible to produce unexpected and unwanted high-pitched squeaks. Most beginners find they are able to make fairly rapid progress on the clarinet. Many players find it an easy instrument to take up after playing the recorder, and the sound is fairly easy to make over the whole range of the instrument. Developing fluency and good intonation is more difficult.

The cost of a new B flat (Bb) clarinet is relatively modest, and there is a good secondhand market. Running costs include occasional maintenance, which should always be undertaken by an experienced technician, and reeds. Beginners seem to eat reeds! Clarinets are not heavy and are easily transportable.

Bassoon

The bassoon developed in Baroque times, taking its place in the orchestra of the Classical period, and although used in military and windbands, is little used in popular music and jazz.

Bassoon players are always in demand! It is an easier instrument to play than the oboe, its double-reed compatriot in the orchestra, and although it can be quite a stretch for the fingers it is usual for beginners to make quite rapid progress. Bassoonists can be sure of a place in any ensemble, providing, as they do, the bass part for a woodwind group. The bassoon is equally at home in an orchestra, windband or wind quintet.

Bassoons are usually played sitting down, although they are found in marching bands. When seated, the player uses either a spike attached to the end of the instrument, or a sling around his/her neck, to take the weight of the instrument off his/her hands and arms. It is also possible to play standing up using a sling, and thus it is possible to march playing a bassoon. Beginners may go through reeds at a considerable rate in the same way as beginner oboists, clarinettists and saxophonists.

Modern beginners' bassoons are made of artificial materials, as are oboes and clarinets. The bassoon is more expensive than a flute, clarinet or oboe, but still modest in cost when compared to a high quality stringed instrument. The purchase price of a bassoon is significant and the secondhand market is weak. Running costs include occasional maintenance, which should always be carried out by an experienced technician, and reeds. Bassoons are quite heavy, and the cases are quite large.

Saxophone

The saxophone is a comparatively modern instrument, having been invented by the Belgian, Adolphe Sax, in the mid-nineteenth century. Most beginners start on the alto or tenor saxophone, but there is a complete family of instruments including soprano, baritone and bass. The alto, tenor and baritone are the most widely used, although the soprano has grown in popularity in recent years.

The saxophone is associated in most people's minds with jazz, although it was invented before jazz evolved. It can therefore be used as a classical instrument or played in a more popular style. It features occasionally in orchestral music: for example, there are saxophone solos in Ravel's 'Bolero', Mussourgsky's 'Pictures at an Exhibition', and Sir William Walton's 'Belshazzar's Feast', but it is most at home in the windband, jazz big band or jazz ensemble.

The saxophone combines a clarinet-like mouthpiece with a conical metal body, and despite having a metal body is classed as a member of the woodwind family of instruments. The sound is produced quite readily, and playing notes over the full range of the instrument is not too difficult. It changes register at the octave, like the flute and bassoon, and unlike the clarinet, which changes register at the twelfth note of the scale. The octave register change means that the fingerings are almost exactly the same for lower and higher notes. Saxophonists wear a strap or sling, which enables them to take the weight of the instrument on their shoulders rather than their arms, so they can play sitting or standing.

The saxophone is an attractive instrument for beginners and also for clarinettists, who often move over to it after a year or two, finding it similar to play. The nature of its construction means that the holes are covered by parts of the mechanism, rather than the fingers, in a similar way to the flute. This means that the size of the player's hand is almost immaterial, and for beginners this can be quite an advantage. The flute shares this feature, whereas clarinet, oboe and bassoon do not. The alto saxophone in E flat (Eb) is the most popular for beginners. The fingering for all saxophones is essentially the same, although the technique for producing the sound varies.

The purchase price is relatively modest, and there is a strong secondhand market for saxophones. This is due in part to the number of children who are attracted to the instrument but give up when they find that, like most instruments, it is never quite as easy as a professional player makes it look. Running costs include occasional maintenance, a sling or strap, and reeds.

Smaller Woodwind Instruments
Smaller woodwind instruments for beginners include the curved-head flute, the fife, chalumeau, C clarinet and teneroon, amongst many others.

A number of woodwind instruments are available in slightly modified formats to suit the needs of young beginners. This may mean a reduction in size or keywork, or both, or some other form of simplification. Although primarily intended as a way of introducing these instruments to children, there is no real reason why, as an adult, you shouldn't consider trying one of these formats as a simpler and cheaper way of finding out if this is the direction you want to go in. That said, and as with any other instrument, make sure your chosen teacher is happy with this idea as well. If they are not familiar with these instruments, or don't like using them for beginners, you may find yourself having to search for another teacher before even getting properly started.

The curved-head flute simply shortens the reach that the player needs to cover the holes. In all other respects it is the same as a traditional flute.

The fife originated in Europe in the Renaissance, and is often used in marching and military bands. In recent years it has been used to introduce beginners to the flute. The sound is made in a similar way to the flute, but the fife is a smaller instrument and has no keywork, thus making it easier for beginners.

The chalumeau is a simple version of the clarinet. It is recorder sized, uses recorder fingering and has no keywork, but does use a normal B flat clarinet mouthpiece and reed. The C clarinet is also available in a format called the clarineo, and was formerly called the Lyons C. This is a slightly simplified version of a traditional clarinet, but with some reduction in the keywork and pitched in C.

The teneroon was a smaller version of the bassoon used in Renaissance times, but is a fairly recent development and is a smaller version of the traditional bassoon. It is pitched a fifth higher and made with reduced keywork. Its overall smaller size enables younger children to reach and cover all the holes.

Although these instruments were designed principally with children in mind, there is nothing to stop you, as an adult, buying, renting or borrowing one, to try it out. This may give you a feeling for whether you're going in the right direction with your choice of instrument, and if not, it could make a musical present for a family member.

KEYBOARD INSTRUMENTS

The family of keyboard instruments includes the pianoforte, usually referred to as a piano, which is often regarded as a percussion instru-

Harpichord. NAHARIYANI

Grand piano.

BOB ORSILLO

Synthesizer.

OLEKSIY MARK

Pipe organ. FOTOLUMINATE LLC

ment as the action of depressing the keys makes the hammers hit the strings; electronic keyboards of various categories; harpsichord and organ. Grand, upright and electric pianos all have a single set of black and white keys, usually eighty-eight in total, covering seven octaves.

Keyboard instruments involve a number of complex skills. First, there is the need for manual dexterity, although it is possible to play keyboard instruments with some restrictions on finger movement. Second is the expectation that both hands will develop independence and strength. Third, that keyboard music is usually written on two staves, which each allocate different lines and spaces to different note names. This is multi-tasking on a grand scale, and on the organ there is all of this, plus several manuals (keyboards), and a pedal board requiring independent movement of each foot.

Making matters worse is the fact that many good pianists make it look easy. They seem able to look away from the keyboard, perhaps taking in the audience and smiling at them too. The answer is, of course, practice, and a lot of it. Electronic keyboards can make things a little easier by doing some of the hard work for the player, but aspiring keyboard players should be in no doubt that, while on the piano it is easy to make the sound as compared, say, to an oboe or French horn, the accumulation of skills required to perform a difficult piece on a keyboard should not be underestimated.

Pianos

The pianoforte was developed at the beginning of the eighteenth century as the successor to the fortepiano, which had leather-covered hammers and thin harpsichord-like strings. The piano's basic form has changed little since the middle of the nineteenth century, although the twentieth century has seen the development of a broader range of instruments including, for example, small mini uprights and acoustic/electronic instruments.

The manufacture of pianos was traditionally centred in mainland Europe, and at the beginning of the twentieth century there were no fewer than 100 piano makes in Camden Town, London, alone. Today there are hardly any manufacturers left in the UK, and production is now concentrated in China, where the market for pianos and lessons far outstrips the rest of the world.

The past thirty years have seen a considerable increase in the development, manufacture and sales of small upright pianos designed for houses and flats. More recently made small uprights often include a practice pedal which presses a felt bar against the strings that further reduces their volume. So-called 'silent' pianos are also available, which can be played normally, or electronically, with the player listening to the results on headphones.

The piano is used in all kinds of ensemble music-making, and as a solo instrument. The repertoire for piano is enormous. It can also be used to play music originally composed for other instruments. A facility on the piano therefore gives access to a very, very wide range of compositions in all musical styles. For many learners and musicians who specialize in other instruments it becomes a second instrument, and has been described as the musician's 'maid-of-all-work'. Although the piano is a difficult instrument to play well, albeit an easy instrument on which to make a sound, most beginners can make relatively rapid progress. Pianists have the advantage of not having to take their instrument with them, and the disadvantage of having to play on whatever instrument is provided for them.

The purchase price for a secondhand piano is relatively modest, and the market is strong. Pianos often appear in auctions, and there are also specialist piano-only auctions held regularly around the country. When buying secondhand it is important for you to check that the instrument is either in tune, or capable of being tuned, to what is known as 'concert pitch': in other words, A = 440hz. This is particularly important if you plan to use your piano to play music with other instruments or voices.

An equally practical consideration when looking at secondhand instruments is to ensure the absence of active woodworm. Pianos have a life expectancy of thirty to one hundred years or more, so capital cost should be considered against that time frame when purchasing an instrument. A good quality, older instrument may well be worth purchasing with a view to spending a significant sum on refurbishment. There are plenty of reliable and well informed piano dealers who will be able to provide sound, practical advice on the best purchase you could make for your anticipated musical needs. A small upright piano weighs about 200kg (440lb), so can be accommodated in most homes without too much difficulty. Experienced piano movers can tackle flights of stairs, and if necessary, pianos can sometimes be delivered to your home through upper-floor windows. Grand pianos come in various sizes from 'baby' through to 275cm (5–9ft) for a full size concert grand. It's worth bearing in mind that a good quality upright may produce a better sound than a baby grand of poorer quality. Running costs include occasional maintenance and regular tuning. As a rule of thumb, the older the upright, the larger it will be.

Harpsichord

The harpsichord makes a sound by pressing down the keys which causes the 'jacks' to pluck, rather than hit, the strings. Harpsichords and organs usually have more than one set of keys or manuals, the term being used to distinguish the keys depressed by the fingers from the foot-operated pedals found on both instruments. The harpsichord was the household instrument that came before the piano, which took its place from the classical period onwards. It is a sensitive instrument and requires frequent tuning, so it is unlikely to be ideal for an absolute beginner. It is at its best playing music composed with its sound in mind, whereas a piano can more readily accommodate having music of any period played on it.

Organ

Organs, whether the electronic sort or the blown-air variety commonly found in churches, usually have one or more keyboards, called manuals, and a pedalboard as well. Pipe or blown-air organs are found in most churches, and electronic organs are often played for light entertainment or as part of a jazz ensemble.

In order to play the organ well you will need to develop a technical prowess very similar to that of a pianist, and ideally you will also need to develop independent footwork in order to operate the organ's pedals. Church organs have a pedalboard much like a keyboard, and also often have numerous pedals which enable the sounds produced to be changed without interruption to the playing. The electronic organ grew in popularity before the development of the electronic keyboard. The latter, which is more portable, is usually the more popular choice today. One advantage of the electronic organ is that its built-in technology allows you to perform a seemingly sophisticated piece almost from the outset as it can provide additional harmony, an accompaniment and rhythmic backing.

Playing the blown-air organ almost certainly means practising in a church. There is an implicit restriction, to some extent, on the styles of music you are likely to study. Organists usually begin as piano students, and then perhaps, if spending time in a church choir or even as a choral scholar, become interested in the church organ as an instrument in its own right. Church organs do not move! Electronic organs can be moved but are not designed to be moved frequently.

Electronic Keyboards and Synthesizers

There are a number of sub-groups within this category. First, the electric piano is simply an electronic instrument that makes a sound as near to a 'real' piano sound as possible. A good electronic piano is much cheaper than its equivalent acoustic instrument, has the advantages of portability, and no need for regular tuning, along with being able to be listened to through headphones. Although the 'touch' will never be quite the same as its acoustic counterpart, it may include features such as the ability to record yourself playing, and provide a range of differing sounds to choose from, and even offer a range of different sampled piano sounds, so it is definitely worthy of consideration.

The electronic keyboard may be categorized as a synthesizer or workstation, and will often have five octaves (sixty-one keys) rather than the full eighty-eight keys of an acoustic piano. It will also have the capacity to play a huge range of built-in sounds and rhythmic accompaniments, as well as allowing the player to edit and layer the sounds it makes.

There is a huge range of electronic keyboards available, from very modestly priced instruments, to those costing several thousands of pounds. In order to play any of them fluently you will need to develop a basic keyboard technique, and many, if not all, teachers would recommend starting on an acoustic piano, organ or electric piano. There are teachers who specialize in electronic keyboards, so make sure you have the right teacher for your chosen instrument and musical aspirations.

PERCUSSION

Percussion includes orchestral percussion, drumkit, snare drum, cajon, djembe, salsa, marimba and vibraphone. This section highlights just a few members of the percussion family.

Marimba. ANTON HAVELAAR

Drumkit. MIKHAIL BAKUNOVICH

Djembe.
AZRISURATMIN

Vibraphone. FURTSEFF

Learning a percussion instrument may be the least favourite choice for family and neighbours, but that shouldn't prevent you from following your dream. Most beginners start by establishing some basic stick technique, and perhaps music-reading as well, just using a snare drum. Although an acoustic instrument makes quite a large sound, a practice pad is an acceptable substitute for a snare drum in terms of developing stick technique, but as a learner you may need to be disciplined in order to be satisfied with its lack of authentic sound. An electronic kit could be the answer, but may be much more expensive. However, check that your teacher is happy with any of this before going ahead.

Many people learning the drum kit simply want to play the pieces they already know, so may see little point in learning to read from notation. This could be judged as a false economy, and it is important to check that your teacher can read music as well as drum notation, and that he/she will teach music reading as part of the process of learning the instrument, if you really want to study in depth.

The orchestral percussionist is expected to handle everything from drum kit to timpani, sometimes referred to as kettledrums, triangle, cymbals, bass drum, glockenspiel, marimba and even piano, along with many more besides. This range of expertise can only be acquired over a period of time, and usually involves mastering snare-drum basics as the foundation of study and stick technique.

Marimba and vibraphone are just two of the many melodic percussion instruments, and can be completely satisfying to play in their own right without any additional instrumentation or accompaniment. Both instruments take up quite a bit of space and it would be wise to listen to and look at them, perhaps arranging a trial play on your chosen one, before considering a purchase.

Playing a broad range of percussion instruments demands a variety of skills and a development of expertise that is on a par with any other instrument or family of instruments. The kit player is responsible for keeping the band in time, and almost all percussion parts require a clear conviction of purpose that enables the player to come in, on the right note, at the right time. Whilst this conviction of purpose is shared with all instruments, it is much more noticeable on a loud percussion instrument than on a quieter woodwind, if a false entry is made.

Snare Drum (Side Drum)

Every percussionist starts with the snare or side drum, which allows you to learn basic stick technique, rhythmic patterns and reading percussion notation, which is slightly different to the more usual stave-based notation.

The snare drum, a twin-headed drum, is used in numerous musical contexts from drum corps to marching bands to orchestras, and of course is a key component of the drumkit used in pop music, jazz and other combos. It is typically played with sticks, but wire or nylon brushes can also be used to vary the range of sounds it can produce. It originated from the tabor drum, which accompanied the flute. As its use spread through the military, it was used as a way of signalling to troops, until it was superseded by the bugle. The drumheads on a snare drum were originally made of calf skin, but the move to plastic heads began in the 1950s. The snares are a group of thin wires stretched from one side of the drum to the other across the underneath non-playing surface. From this single instrument you may move on to using a practice pad or an electronic or acoustic kit.

Cajon

Cajon means box, and this drum originated in Peru. It is a six-sided box which is played by slapping the front or rear faces with the hands, fingers or sometimes percussion sticks such as brushes or mallets. The player sits astride the box and strikes the thinnest surface, made of plywood. It is made in a variety of sizes, and in recent years has become popular in schools where a set can be used for a whole class lesson. Some are made with built-in snares to increase the variety of sounds attainable.

Djembe

Many beginners now start in percussion groups on djembe, a goblet-shaped drum from West Africa, which is played with the bare hands. It is popular in schools, where djembe are often used for whole class instrumental lessons, and can produce a wide range of sounds. In its original context it is only played by men, and can be used to tell a story. It is an ideal instrument to start your musical experience with, and playing rhythms with a group of learners really helps to establish an understanding of pulse and rhythm.

Salsa

Like the djembe, salsa drumming is often used for whole class instrumental lessons in schools. However, you may find opportunities to join an adult beginners' group. Like the djembe, the drums are played with your hands. But the term refers more to musical style than the instruments themselves. Salsa is also a lively form of dance, and the music-making originates from Latin America.

Marimba

The marimba consists of a set of wooden bars arranged like a piano keyboard, which are struck with mallets to produce the sounds. Resonators attached to the bars amplify their sound. The instrument has its origin in Africa, and has a lower and more resonant sound than the xylophone. In recent years it has become used increasingly in scoring for television themes, advertisements and film music, so becoming a very familiar sound. The most common sizes have a range of four to five octaves, but there is no fixed size.

Vibraphone

This instrument was made famous to one generation by jazzman Lionel Hampton. It is similar in appearance to the marimba and xylophone, with resonator tubes suspended beneath its metal bars. The key difference is that each resonator has a fan or butterfly at the upper end mounted on a metal shaft driven by an electronic motor. The speed of rotation of the fans gives the vibraphone its characteristic 'vibrato' sound. It is an instrument that was developed during the twentieth century, and jazz drummer Lionel Hampton, who took up the vibraphone in the 1930s, brought the instrument to public notice through his recordings. The instrument also appears in classical music.

TRADITIONAL INSTRUMENTS

Traditional instruments include fiddle, concertina, accordion, pipes, mouth organ (harmonica) and hammered dulcimer.

Accordion. LANTAPIX

Concertina.
NAHARIYANI

Dulcimer. PETR JILEK

Harmonica. MORGAN SILVESTER ART

These instruments are associated with traditional music, and are closely related to those used in Western classical music. They are part of a large group of instruments used in traditional music-making, and the ones featured here are no more than a few of the more commonly played ones. They will have a special appeal for some learners, which is likely to have been stimulated by your encounters with music-making in this genre, perhaps from your earliest years. Tuition will be most readily available in parts of the country where there is a thriving tradition of traditional or folk-music. However, if not apparently readily available, it is worth some internet exploration, which may reveal traditional music activity in your neighbourhood, and access to the network of musicians and teachers that are involved.

Fiddle

The term 'fiddle' is used to describe a violin played as a traditional musical instrument, and interestingly, most professional violinists refer to their instrument as their 'fiddle'. It may have minor differences in construction from an orchestral violin, but essentially it is the same.

Repertoire for the fiddle, as with most traditional instruments, depends on the location and cultural heritage of the indigenous population. There are as many different performance styles as there are countries that have folk fiddlers.

The instrument is usually played in a similar fashion to the classical violin, although bow hold can be different, and in some folk-fiddle traditions the instrument is held lower down the body rather than under the chin. Traditional fiddles tend to thrive in communities where there is an active folk-music tradition. It may be taught in a similar way to the classical violin in either one-to-one or small group lessons, or as part of an ensemble experience similar to the brass-band tradition. Most folk music thrives on an aural learning tradition which emphasizes memorization of the music to be performed, having learned it aurally, with little or no recourse to notation. Working within such a tradition is fine and admirable, but remember that if you wish to hold your own in orchestras or bands, you may need to develop music-reading skills to match your aural skills. It is also probable that the playing techniques needed for each tradition will be slightly different, so they may become mutually exclusive.

Purchase and maintenance costs are modest, and the same as for the orchestral/classical violin, and of course, fiddles are light and easy to carry and available in a wide range of sizes.

Concertina

The concertina is a melody instrument, invented in the early nineteenth century by an Englishman, Charles Wheatstone, and around the same time, and probably independently, in Germany. There are numerous variations on the basic instrument, which has been a popular and widely accepted addition to traditional music-making. The instrument's core repertoire is the traditional music of the region and the peoples where it is played.

The concertina is described as a free-reed instrument, and is played using two hands to squeeze the bellows, which then force air through a reed to generate the sound. You press buttons at the end of the instrument to make different notes, and the instrument is usually chromatic. As with other traditional instruments, teaching and learning the concertina may follow different models to the other orchestral and band instruments. It has the advantage of being highly portable. It was at its height of popularity in the mid-nineteenth century, but then there was a gradual decline in interest from the early twentieth century. The revival of interest in folk and traditional music in the mid-twentieth century led to a resurgence of interest in the concertina.

New concertinas can be relatively expensive, but fortunately there is a big secondhand market. It is essential to take advice from a player, collector or teacher before purchasing a secondhand instrument. Concertinas are fairly robust and do not require a huge amount of maintenance apart from occasional repairs to the bellows and adjustment to the reeds.

Accordion

The accordion was developed in the early nineteenth century and may be associated in many people's minds with Parisian street cafés. It is an example of a free-reed instrument, where the sound is produced by air being forced through the reed that is located within the body of the instrument. There are numerous variations on the instrument's basic theme, and as with most things, expenditure will dictate, to some extent, the level of sophistication.

The accordion is associated with both a folk and popular tradition, but also attracts many serious 'classical' composers, particularly outside the UK, and features in music by Tchaikovsky and the American, Charles Ives. Where it is used to play traditional music, the repertoire is likely to be influenced by the location.

The accordion is played by compression and expansion of the bellows. Different notes are played on a piano-like keyboard, usually with the right hand, and chord buttons are pressed with the left hand. The number of black and white keys varies with the size of the accordion, and is usually in the range of twenty-five to forty-five.

The accordion, although widely spread across the world, is not commonly taught in the UK other than by private teachers. Playing the instrument involves a degree of physical strength to manipulate the bellows, and also a high degree of co-ordination to enable each hand to function independently, whilst maintaining the necessary bellows movement.

Instruments vary widely in price, but a good instrument can be obtained for a modest outlay. There is a steady secondhand market, and an expert's advice should be sought before attempting a purchase. Maintenance and running costs are modest.

Pipes

Pipes include the Northumbrian small pipes, Border pipes and Highland bagpipes.

There are many different varieties of bagpipe, but they all work on the same principles. The Northumbrian small pipes are the quietest and most gentle sounding, with the full Highland bagpipes being intended very much as an outdoor instrument.

The pipes are melodic instruments and are usually tuned to a different scale from that used for most Western instruments. The instrument consists of a bag, which you fill with air by blowing through a pipe to fill it. You then squeeze the bag, forcing the air through a fixed reed which looks a bit like the double reed of a bassoon, and use the chanter to play different notes, by covering or uncovering holes with your fingers.

The Highland pipes are intended for outdoor use and practice can be accomplished indoors by using a modestly priced practice chanter, or a more expensive electronic bagpipe substitute. This may well be important for family harmony and neighbourhood peace. The smaller pipes produce a less penetrating more mellow tune and can be more readily tolerated indoors.

Northumbrian pipes are the least expensive. Maintenance for all pipes includes looking after the reeds and air sack. Highland pipes are the biggest, but all pipes are available in different sizes to accommodate individuals' needs.

Mouth Organ: Harmonica

The harmonica is a free-reed instrument. The compact harmonica or mouth organ was developed in the early nineteenth century by the Englishman, Charles Wheatstone, who invented the concertina.

It features in rhythm and blues bands, Country and Western music, and in a range of styles, and is found all around the world.

The instrument's sound is associated in the minds of many people with the rhythm and blues bands of the 1960s on the one hand, and the virtuoso playing of performers in the classical style, such as the late Larry Adler, on the other. You blow into the instrument to produce one pitch, and draw air from the instrument to produce another pitch.

Formal teaching may not be very widely available, but as a teach-yourself instrument it has great potential for adult learners who want something a little different. As with other blown instruments, it should not be shared. It is undoubtedly highly portable, very modestly priced for a basic model, and very versatile. The most familiar model is pocket sized, but it can be bigger, as a whole family of instruments is available. Like a number of other instruments, the harmonica has been used in the past few years as a whole class instrument for beginner instrumentalists.

Hammered Dulcimer

The hammered dulcimer is found in a variety of sizes and tunings around the world. It consists of wire strings, usually tuned in pairs, stretched across a wooden frame, and the sound is made by hitting the strings with small wooden hammers or mallets. Its sound is distinctive and appealing, but tuning is a problem where the instrument has a traditional wooden frame. Contemporary versions often use a steel frame to provide more stability. In Eastern Europe one of its descendants is the cimbalom, which is also used in classical music – for example, *Háry János* by the Hungarian composer Kodaly.

INDIAN CLASSICAL MUSIC

Indian classical music includes the instruments tabla, harmonium and sitar.

The focus of this book is mainly on the instruments associated with music in Western European culture over the past eight hundred years. However, the UK is very much a multi-ethnic society, so we now have ready access to music from many parts of the world. As our familiarity with music from other cultures increases, there has been a steady growth in interest from adults who would like to explore music from a culture other than the one into which they were born. Aside from any difficulties with unfamiliarity in terms of the instrument and its musical genre, the key issue to be

Indian musical instruments.
Sitar and tabla

Indian musical instruments: sitar and tabla.

Indian harmonium. SMILEUS

considered is the role that the music created by this instrument, plays in its home culture.

Learning to play a musical instrument is not merely a matter of understanding the mechanical processes associated with producing sounds on that instrument. It is, crucially, being able to give expression and meaning to music as it is played on that instrument. Effective teachers teach music through the instrument, whatever the genre and culture, rather than merely teaching technical mastery of the instrument.

The following instruments come from Indian classical music, which is usually divided into two major traditions: Hindustani music of northern India, and Karnatak (Carnatic) music of southern India, although many regions of India also have their own musical traditions that are independent of these. Both traditions use a system of ragas or sets of pitches for composing melodies, and talas for rhythms.

Tabla

The tabla is a popular percussion instrument widely used in all styles of North Indian music. The instrument consists of a pair of tuned, single-headed, hand-played drums, and these are made in different sizes. Tabla is the name given to the higher-pitched drum of the two. The tabla player performs classical music from northern India.

Players sit on the floor and play one drum with their strongest, or dominant hand, and the other drum with the other hand. Different sounds are made by using different parts of the hand: thumbs, fingers, knuckle joints and so on. The player tunes his instrument to suit the other instruments in an ensemble.

If you choose an instrument from a different cultural origin to your own, you may find learning to play it more difficult, for the simple reason that the music itself is less familiar than that of your own culture. This does not preclude you learning the instrument, nor should it be seen as an insurmountable barrier, but it should be considered at the outset. Tabla are modestly priced, and are available in different sizes, so can be chosen to match the needs of the learner. Running costs are likewise modest.

Harmonium

The term 'harmonium' is used to describe all pedal-pumped, free-reed instruments. The American and European harmonium is akin to an upright piano, and is often associated with churches and the drawing rooms of the Victorian era. The Indian version of the harmonium, derived from the American/European model, is much smaller and easily portable, and is hand-operated rather than pedal-pumped.

There is a fair amount of original nineteenth-century sheet music available for the Western harmonium, including concert solo and orchestral music, but the instrument has since declined in popularity. On the other hand, the Indian instrument still features prominently in Indian classical music today, and music is written and arranged for it. With the Western harmonium, you fill the bellows with air by using foot pedals. To play the Indian harmonium the player usually sits on the floor to play it, and it is usually played with one hand while the player pumps the bellows with the other.

The Western harmonium is rarely, if ever, taught these days. What was once a source of fascination was initially superseded by the growth in availability of modestly priced pianos, and subsequently the piano was overtaken by the wonders of the home electronic organ, and now the electronic keyboard. The Victorian harmonium is not an ideal instrument to recommend for a beginner, but in contrast, its Indian counterpart is gaining in popularity. The portable Indian harmonium is available as a modestly priced instrument, which is surprisingly robust, with low maintenance costs.

Sitar

The sitar is considered to be the most popular Indian classical musical instrument, and has become more widely known in the West since the 1960s. It is a melodic rather than a chordal instrument, and its Western equivalent is the lute. The neck and soundboard are made of wood, and the body was originally a gourd, a hollowed and dried pumpkin.

The traditional music played on the sitar is Indian classical music, and is improvised and heartfelt. The emotional quality is provided not just by the sequence of notes played, but also by the small inflections, or changes in pitch, given to each note.

The sitar is a difficult instrument to both tune and play. It has up to twenty strings, of which up to six or seven are used to play, with typically four active ones. The remaining strings are called 'sympathetic' because they vibrate in sympathy with those struck by the player. Some of the sympathetic strings function as drones. The active strings are plucked with a metallic plectrum worn on the index finger, and the player sits on the floor. The notes are far apart so the hands need to move up and down a lot, and the action is high, requiring strong fingers to press down on the strings. Finding the right fret is also difficult.

Learning the sitar is a lifelong project and cultural experience. Sitars may appeal most to adults from a cultural background matching the origin of the instrument. Learning to play it will mean learning to know and understand Indian classical music.

Even a sitar suitable for a beginner is relatively expensive, and as with most instruments, price increases with quality. Running costs are also high, as replacement strings are not cheap. Sitars require regular cleaning and tuning.

Let me count you in

With anything new, there is that moment when you either leave it on the shelf, or you just have to do it. In fact it rather depends on your preferred learning style, because you may already have begun to learn an instrument before even taking a look at this book, or you may be spending a huge amount of time doing research before you make any firm commitment.

If you have already done a lot of thinking and have weighed up the pros and cons, please keep in mind that making music is a completely natural thing to do. You may be a gifted individual to whom playing music comes very naturally, or you may find it quite a struggle. Either way, it is the right thing for you to do, and there is very little likelihood of any harm coming to anyone as a result of your explorations of this fascinating art form.

If you are able to join a singing group of some sort, even for a few weeks, it will give you an opportunity to experience music-making at first hand, or better still, choose an inexpensive instrument such as a harmonica, ocarina, recorder or ukulele, or something similar which is low cost and which you can experiment with at home. The internet will provide some tuition, and no one else need know that you are doing this, if you want to keep your enthusiasm under wraps at this stage.

If you are approaching retirement, it is probable that you will come to a point when you have more time on your hands, and taking up a musical instrument will provide the ideal opportunity to devote some of it, or all of it, to something that you've always wanted to do. Once you start, it's a task that will never be complete because there's always another piece of music to master or a technical skill or a reading challenge, so you will never run out of things to do.

Furthermore as much as music-making will give you and others some pleasure, it also has health benefits, especially for older adults. It can help to lower your blood pressure, decrease your heart rate, reduce stress, and lessen anxiety and depression – even if you experience some frustration making your chosen instrument produce the sounds you want it to.

Then again, you could be another Alan Rusbridger, the former editor of *The Guardian*, who wrote the book *Play it Again* (see Recommended Reading). In the summer of 2010, he set himself the formidable challenge of learning, within a year, Chopin's first ballade in G minor, which he would play from memory. He had always been a keen amateur pianist and clarinettist, but this piece by Chopin really is a significant challenge for someone in their forties who has done very little music-making for some fifteen years because of the immense demands of their high-profile job. He describes the experience as being about a re-awakening of a desire to play the piano, and Rusbridger's account is a reminder to us all that anything is possible with perseverance.

Whatever you decide to do, you are very unlikely to regret entering the world of music-making, perhaps for the very first time and taking the opportunity to create and communicate through the medium of sound or re-discovering its pleasures after a number of years' absence. It's a sociable world with a gentle edge of competition.

Glossary

accompaniment   A pianist may play the piano to provide an accompaniment for any instrument – for example the violin, clarinet or trumpet in a piece of music such as a sonata – or to provide the accompaniment for a singer. An orchestra may play the accompaniment in a concerto composed for solo instrument with orchestra.

aerophone   An instrument where wind is the primary source of sound production.

alto   The lower-pitched mature female voice. The term is also used to denote instruments of certain pitch ranges in instrumental families, for example alto saxophone, alto flute.

Baroque   Refers to a period in the arts from about 1600–1750, and the style that dominated that period. Bach and Handel were Baroque composers. The word derives from the Portuguese.

Baritone   The mature male singing voice with a range between tenor and bass. The term is also used to describe lower-pitched instruments in a family, for example baritone saxophone.

bass   The lowest-sounding mature male voice. The term is also used to denote instruments of certain pitch ranges in instrumental families, for example bass clarinet, bass trombone.

bass clef   A sign placed at the beginning of a stave which indicates which pitches are to be associated with each line and space.

chordophone   An instrument where the sound is made by plucking, or drawing a bow across strings.

chromatic   In Western music, the smallest pitch interval between notes in terms of instrument design and construction is the semitone. On the piano all the keys are one semitone away from the next adjacent key, be it black or white. A chromatic scale moves up or down one semitone at a time. Within an octave there are twelve semitones.

Classical Refers to a period in the arts from about 1750–1830, and the style that dominated that period. Mozart and Haydn were Classical composers. The word is often used to denote 'serious' or 'non-popular' music.

concerto Most commonly used to define a piece of music for solo instrument, usually with orchestral accompaniment. The solo concerto developed in the Classical period.

concert pitch A440. This means that on a piano, the note A above middle C is tuned to 440 Hertz. This pitch was standardized in 1948. Prior to that, individual instrument makers worked to the pitch they preferred. With the rise of the orchestra in the nineteenth century, and the increased mobility of instrumentalists, the need for standardization became paramount.

conservatoire (conservatory) A music conservatoire is a music school or college where students work to a very high standard: for example, the Royal College of Music and Royal Academy of Music in London are both conservatoires.

consort A group of instruments. A whole consort means all from the same family, and a broken consort consists of different instruments.

diatonic scale A scale of seven notes made up of five whole tone intervals and two semitone intervals. Major and minor scales are examples.

dynamics The range of volume used in the performance or notation of a piece of music.

electrophone Generic term used for electronic instruments.

embouchure The shaping of the mouth and lips to accommodate and play a brass-wind or woodwind instrument.

ensembles (some of the more commonplace ones):

brass band A musical ensemble consisting principally of brass instruments with some percussion.

band Any musical ensemble!

military band instruments played by soldiers. A military band is capable of playing music for ceremonial occasions and will play whilst marching. It includes woodwind, brass and percussion instruments.

orchestra A musical ensemble that usually includes string, woodwind, brass and percussion instruments. The term is derived from the Greek name for the area in front of the stage reserved for the chorus.

recorder consort A group of recorders including instruments across the whole range of the family from high-pitched sopranino to the low-pitched great bass. The term is associated with the heyday of the instrument in the sixteenth century, although it is still applied today.

recorder group The modern version of a recorder consort, which may not include so many members of this family of instruments. Many schools have a recorder group, or recorder ensemble, rather than a consort.

string quartet Four members of the string family: two violins, one viola and one 'cello. Each plays a separate part, and the violins are identified as first and second. The first violin is the leader of the quartet, and the part written for this instrument will, overall, be of higher notes than the second violin part.

wind quintet Four members of the woodwind family and one brass instrument. The standard wind quintet consists of flute, oboe, clarinet, French horn and bassoon.

windband (wind orchestra, symphonic windband) An ensemble of woodwind, brass and percussion instruments, which can range from forty to eighty players and is the equivalent of the orchestra, but without strings.

falsetto A singing technique that enables the mature male voice to sing in notes of the alto or soprano range.

flat A musical sign, rather like a lower case 'b', which when placed in front of a note on the stave indicates that the note should be played one semitone lower.

flautist A flute player.

glissando A continuous slide from one pitch to another.

Guidonian hand Developed in the eleventh century by Guido d'Arrezzo, in which he assigned each part of the hand a note. With his development of the stave these were the forerunners of modern musical notation.

harmonic series When a column of air or a single string vibrates, it is said to produce its 'fundamental note'. In fact the string or air also vibrates simultaneously in smaller portions, each producing one note in the harmonic series. It is the relative strength or weakness of these harmonics as produced by any given instrument that give that particular instrument its characteristic sound or timbre. In other words, it is what makes an oboe sound different from clarinet.

idiophone An instrument in which the sound is produced from the instrument itself (e.g. maracas).

jazz A genre of music that originated in African-American communities during the late nineteenth and early twentieth centuries.

Kodaly, Zoltan (1882–1967) A Hungarian composer and music educator who developed an approach to music education that is based on teaching, learning and understanding music, through the experience of singing. Composer of *Háry János*, which features the cimbalom.

madrigal A setting of text for several voices, a form that originated in Italy and blossomed in England during the reign of Elizabeth I (1588–1693). Singers may have been accompanied by instruments such as the lute and viols.

Medieval The period in history from c500–1400AD.

membranophone An instrument in which the sound is produced by vibrating a stretched membrane.

Minimalism Late twentieth-century compositional style with reduced musical materials often achieved through repetition.

modes During the Medieval and Renaissance periods music was generally composed in one of eight modes. Our modern major and minor scales are two examples of these modes.

natural A musical sign, which when placed in front of a note on the stave indicates that the note should be played without sharpening or flattening it. The sign often cancels the effect of a sharp or flat placed in the music a few notes before the naturalized one.

notation A means of expressing musical sounds in written format so that individuals other than the composer can recreate the composition. There are many different forms of notation besides the five-line stave, which may be the most familiar.

orchestra (*see* **ensemble**)

Orff, Carl (1895–1982) German composer and music educator best known for *Carmina Burana*, written in 1937, and for developing the Orff Schulwerk (Music for Children) teaching methodology, which, with its use of classroom percussion instruments, allowed children easy access to composition, improvisation and so on.

perfect pitch The ability to recognize a note by its pitch name, without having another note to which reference may be made.

phrasing Western classical music is composed and played in phrases, which may be indicated by phrase marks in the notation, rather like the clauses in a sentence.

pitch A musical sound has a given pitch. Each key on a piano plays a note of a particular pitch.

plectrum A small plastic device for plucking or strumming some stringed instruments, for example a guitar.

practice An essential part of learning to play an instrument. There are no short cuts and daily practice is advisable.

reed The piece of cane, metal or synthetic material that vibrates and sets a column of air in motion, thus producing a sound. Clarinets and saxophones have a single reed, oboes and bassoon a double reed, accordions, harmonicas and bagpipes enclosed reeds.

relative pitch Relating one note to another. Most musicians, when given the name and pitch of one note, will be able to identify the name and pitch of a second note from the first.

Renaissance The period in history from about 1400–1600.

Romantic A period in the arts from about 1850–1920, and the style that dominated that period. Brahms and Tchaikovsky were Romantic composers.

scales A set of musical notes ordered by pitch.

sharp A musical sign, very like a hashtag, which when placed in front of a note on the stave indicates that the note should be played one semitone higher.

sonata A form in instrumental music which developed in the Baroque and is most commonly associated with the Classical era.

soprano A high-pitched female mature voice; also used to denote instruments of certain pitch ranges in instrumental families, for example soprano saxophone.

stave The five lines upon which Western music is notated, sometimes known as a staff.

Suzuki, Shinichi (1898–1998) A twentieth-century Japanese music educator who developed a teaching method that emphasizes the development of aural skills in advance of music-reading skills.

symphony An extended composition for orchestra, usually in several parts or movements. The word comes from the Greek and means 'a sounding together'.

tablature (tab) A form of notation that shows finger positions rather than pitch; it is used primarily for fretted, stringed instruments such as the guitar or lute. It was in common usage in Renaissance and Baroque times, and is widely used in popular music today.

tenor A high-pitched male mature voice; it is also used to denote instruments of certain pitch ranges in instrumental families, for example tenor trombone, tenor saxophone, tenor horn.

terminology Musicians, especially jazz players, or jazzers as they are often known, seem to use quite a lot of their own terms. Here are just a few examples:

Chart A musical score.

Dots   Conventional Western music notation.

Head   Generally used in jazz to refer to the first main theme or tune of a piece.

Horn   A wind instrument, not necessarily a brass one.

Intro   Introduction.

Jazzer   Musician who plays jazz.

Muso   Musician.

Number   A piece of music.

Outro   The final bars of a piece, known as a coda in classical music terminology.

Reeds   Collective term for woodwind players in, for example, a musical theatre show.

Riff   A simple, catchy, repeated phrase.

timbre   The quality of a musical sound, which makes it distinguishable from another sound. For example, it is the timbre of an oboe's sound that makes it different from the same pitched notes played on the clarinet.

transposition   Trumpet, French horn and clarinet are examples of instruments that produce sounds that are transposed, or different from, the written notation.

treble clef   Sign placed at the beginning of a stave indicating which pitches are to be associated with each line and space.

unison   Two or more instruments or voices playing or singing the same note are said to be 'in unison'.

viols   A family of bowed, fretted, stringed instruments, the forerunners of our modern bowed, stringed instruments. Viols have a quieter tone than modern stringed instruments.

virtuoso   A consummate master of musical technique and artistry.

vocal cords or folds   The part of the human voice which makes the sound of speech and music.

Resources

A word about the two lists that follow: recommended reading and some musical organizations.

There is an enormous quantity of published material on music, music education and music teaching and learning. The sample of books provided here is tiny, and is included simply to introduce you to some of the areas you may find interesting, alongside your pursuit of the musical instrument you would like to learn.

Similarly there is an enormous number of music organizations functioning at national level in the UK, each with a focus on various aspects of music, leave alone all the local associations and organizations connected with music-making. You may find help and support on their websites in your pursuit of musicking.

RECOMMENDED READING

Campbell, Don *The Mozart Effect* Hodder & Stoughton (London, 2001).

Dickinson, Peter (ed) *Music Education in Crisis* Boydell Press (Suffolk, 2013).

Ehrlich, Cyril *The Music Profession in Britain since the Eighteenth Century* Clarendon Paperbacks (UK, 1988).

Ehrlich, Cyril *The Piano – a History* Clarendon Paperbacks (UK, 1976).

Gardiner, Howard *Frames of Mind* Perseus Books (New York, 1983).

Green, Barry and Gallwey, Tim *The Inner Game of Music* Pan Books (London, 1987).

Harris, Paul *The Virtuoso Teacher* Faber Music (London, 2012).

Harris, Paul *Simultaneous Learning – The Definitive Guide* Faber Music (London, 2014).

O'Connor, Joseph *Not Pulling Strings* Lambent (London, 1987).

Roset i Llobet, Jaume and Odam, George *The Musician's Body* Guildhall School of Music & Drama and Ashgate Publishing (London, 2007).

Rusbridger, Alan *Play it Again* Jonathan Cape (London, 2013).

Sachs, Oliver *Musicophilia* Random House (New York, 2007).

Small, Christopher *Musicking: The Meanings of Performing and Listening* Wesleyan University Press (USA, 1998).

Swanwick, Keith *Teaching Music Musically* Routledge (London, 1999).

Wright, David C.H. *The Associated Board of the Royal Schools of Music, a Social and Cultural History* Boydell Press (Suffolk, 2013).

SOME MUSICAL ORGANIZATIONS

Action on Hearing Loss
www.actiononhearingloss.org.uk

Asim UK – carnatic music examination board
www.asimuk.com

Associated Board of the Royal Schools of Music   ABRSM
www.abrsm.org

British Flute Society   BFS
www.bfs.org.uk

British Kodaly Academy   BKA
www.britishkodalyacademy.org

British Suzuki Institute   BSI
www.britishsuzuki.org.uk

Clarinet and Saxophone Society www.cassgb.org	CASS
European Guitar Teachers' Association www.egta.co.uk	EGTA
European String Teachers' Association www.estastrings.org.uk	ESTA
European Piano Teachers' Association www.epta-uk.org	EPTA
European Recorder Teachers' Association www.erta.org.uk	ERTA
Incorporated Society of Musicians www.ism.org	ISM
Jazz Services www.jazzservices.org.uk	
Making Music www.makingmusic.org.uk	MM
Music Education Council www.mec.org.uk	MEC
Music Mark www.musicmark.org.uk	MM
Music Masters and Mistresses Association www.mma-online.org.uk	MMA
Music Teachers.co.uk www.musicteachers.co.uk	
Musicians' Union www.musicansunion.org	MU
Rockschool www.rockschool.co.uk	

Royal National Institute of Blind People   RNIB
www.rnib.org.uk

Sangeet Music Exams (Indian Classical music)
www.sangeet-examinations.co.uk

Scottish Association for Music Education   SAME
www.same.org.uk

The Voices Foundation
www.voices.org.uk

Traditional Music and Song Association of Scotland   TMSA
www.tmsa.org.uk

Trinity College London   TCL
www.trinitycollege.com

Index